Digital Painting Techniques

Wallace Jackson

Apress®

Digital Painting Techniques

ISBN-13 (pbk): 978-1-4842-1735-1

ISBN-13 (electronic): 978-1-4842-1736-8

Managing Director: Welmoed Spahr
Lead Editor: Steve Anglin
Technical Reviewer: Chád Darby
Editorial Board: Steve Anglin, Pramila Balan, Louise Corrigan, Jonathan Gennick, Robert Hutchinson, Celestin Suresh John, Michelle Lowman, James Markham, Susan McDermott, Matthew Moodie, Jeffrey Pepper, Douglas Pundick, Ben Renow-Clarke, Gwenan Spearing
Coordinating Editor: Mark Powers
Copy Editor: Karen Jameson
Compositor: SPi Global
Indexer: SPi Global
Artist: SPi Global

Distributed to the book trade worldwide by Springer Science+Business Media New York, 233 Spring Street, 6th Floor, New York, NY 10013. Phone 1-800-SPRINGER, fax (201) 348-4505, e-mail orders-ny@springer-sbm.com, or visit www.springeronline.com. Apress Media, LLC is a California LLC and the sole member (owner) is Springer Science + Business Media Finance Inc (SSBM Finance Inc). SSBM Finance Inc is a Delaware corporation.

For information on translations, please e-mail rights@apress.com, or visit www.apress.com.

Apress and friends of ED books may be purchased in bulk for academic, corporate, or promotional use. eBook versions and licenses are also available for most titles. For more information, reference our Special Bulk Sales–eBook Licensing web page at www.apress.com/bulk-sales.

Any source code or other supplementary materials referenced by the author in this text are available to readers at www.apress.com/9781484217351. For detailed information about how to locate your book's source code, go to www.apress.com/source-code/. Readers can also access source code at SpringerLink in the Supplementary Material section for each chapter.

This book is dedicated to all those members of the open source community who are working so diligently to make professional new media application development software, as well as content development tools, freely available for new media application developers, so that they can utilize these tools to achieve their creative dreams and big financial goals. Last but not least, I dedicate this book to my brilliant father, Parker Jackson, my family, my life-long friends, and my production ranch neighbors, for their constant help, assistance, and those relaxing, Twilight BBQs, underneath the stars of Point Conception.

Contents at a Glance

About the Author xiii

About the Technical Reviewer xv

Acknowledgments xvii

Introduction xlx

■Chapter 1: Digital Painting Software:
Corel Painter and Inkscape 1

■Chapter 2: The Terminology of Digital Painting:
Vector and Raster 13

■Chapter 3: The Foundation of Digital Painting:
Canvas and Brush... 25

■Chapter 4: Digital Painting with Image Tiles:
Patterns and Weaves 37

■Chapter 5: The Hardware of Digital Painting: Tablet and Stylus.... 53

■Chapter 6: Digital Painting with Image Objects: Using Nozzles 63

■Chapter 7: The Mimicry of Digital Painting: Using Quick Clone.... 79

■Chapter 8: The Algorithms of Digital Painting: Plug-In Filters 93

■Chapter 9: The Selection of Digital Painting: Pulling Masks 105

■Chapter 10: The Compositing of Digital Painting:
Using Layers 119

■Chapter 11: The Refinement of Digital Painting:
Photo-Retouching 135

■Chapter 12: The Coloring Book of Digital Painting: Sketching 147

■Chapter 13: The Animation of Digital Painting:
Physics Engines... 161

■Chapter 14: The Customization of Digital Painting:
Brush Design 173

■Chapter 15: The Automation of Digital Painting:
Programming.. 189

■Chapter 16: Publishing Digital Painting:
Content Delivery Platforms.. 203

Index... 211

Contents

About the Author xiii

About the Technical Reviewer xv

Acknowledgments xvii

Introduction xlx

■Chapter 1: Digital Painting Software:
Corel Painter and Inkscape 1

    Downloading and Installing Inkscape 2

        Inkscape.org: Get Inkscape Illustration Software 2

    Corel Painter 2016: Installing the Software 5

        Setting Up Painter 2016: Adding Painter in Taskbar 6

        Enhancing Painter 2016: Installing Brush Packs 9

    Summary 11

■Chapter 2: The Terminology of Digital Painting:
Vector and Raster 13

    Computer Graphics: Raster versus Vector 13

        Basic Vector Shapes: Vertices, Lines, and Curves 14

        Raster Concepts: Pixels, Aspect Ratio, Color, and Alpha 15

    Inkscape: Tour of Primary User Interface 22

    Painter: Tour of the Basic User Interface 23

    Summary 24

■Chapter 3: The Foundation of Digital Painting: Canvas and Brush... 25

Inkscape Brush Strokes: Digital Painting 25

Calligraphy Brush Stroke Tool: Basic Style Setting...26

Brush Strokes Configuration: Advanced Settings 28

Painter 2016 Brushes: Dynamic Painting 31

Types of Digital Painting: Painter 2016 Workflows 31

Automatic Painting: Using Painter's Auto-Painting...32

Summary... 35

■Chapter 4: Digital Painting with Image Tiles: Patterns and Weaves.. 37

Inkscape Styles: Stroke, Fill, and Gradient 37

Using GIMP: Creating Your Image Pattern 39

Using Imagery in Painting and Illustration 43

Using Bitmap Images as Fill: Inkscape Pattern Fill...43

Bitmaps in Painting: Painter Patterns and Weaves...46

Summary... 52

■Chapter 5: The Hardware of Digital Painting: Tablet and Stylus.. 53

Digital Painting Hardware: Pen and Tablet 53

Pressure-Sensitive Stylus: Digital Pens for Mobile...54

The Tablet with Pressure and Tilt Sensitive Stylus 55

Touchscreen Tablet with Pressure and Tilt Stylus...57

Installing Digital Painting Hardware Driver 58

Find the Correct Driver: Google Search for Product...58

Installing the Latest Driver: Run as Administrator 60

Summary... 61

■**Chapter 6: Digital Painting with Image Objects: Using Nozzles 63**

Painter Nozzles: Painting with Imagery 63

Creating Nozzles: Using Multiple Layers 66

Creating Vector Shapes in Painter: The Brush Tool 67

Creating a Solid Nozzle Image: Using the Fill Tool 69

Transforms in Painter: Using the Rotate Transform 71

Creating a Nozzle: Group Layers and Make Nozzle 74

Summary 78

■**Chapter 7: The Mimicry of Digital Painting: Using Quick Clone 79**

Digital Painting with Photos: Quick Clone 79

Painting Effects: Enhanced Brush Strokes 88

Summary 91

■**Chapter 8: The Algorithms of Digital Painting: Plug-In Filters 93**

Painter's Pixel Processing: Effects Menu 93

Embossing: Applying Surface Textures in Painter 94

Matching Color Palettes: The Tonal Control Menu 95

Posterizing: Reducing the Colors Used in Artwork 96

Sketching: Finding Edges in an Image with Painter 96

Changing Focus: Color Sharpen Images in Painter 97

Esoterica: Special Effects Using Painter Algorithms 98

High Pass Filter: An Audio Filter Works on Images 99

Creating Pop Art: Using the Pop Art Fill Algorithm 100

Inkscape and HTML5 Filters: SVG Filters 101

Summary 103

■Chapter 9: The Selection of Digital Painting: Pulling Masks 105

Painter Selections: Algorithms or Wands.. 105

Auto Selection: Having Algorithms Select Pixels 106

Selecting What You Don't Want: Invert Selection 107

Saving Selections: Using Your Alpha Channels 108

Manual Selection Sets: Using the Magic Wand Tool 110

Inkscape Selections: Selecting Vectors.. 116

Summary.. 118

■Chapter 10: The Compositing of Digital Painting: Using Layers 119

Painter Layers: The Compositing Pipeline 119

Composite Separation: Seamless Layer Elements 120

Drag and Drop: Changing Composite Layer Order 123

Layer Masks: Adding an Alpha Channel to a Layer 126

Dynamic Plug-In Layers: Special Effects Layers..127

Layer Compositing Blend Modes: Color Algorithms..131

Inkscape: Digital Illustration Compositing 133

Summary.. 134

■Chapter 11: The Refinement of Digital Painting: Photo-Retouching 135

Painter Photo-Retouching: Details Editing 135

Rubber Stamp: Sampling Pixels from Another Area 136

The Dodge Tool: Lightening Underneath the Eye 138

The Burn Tool: Darkening the Whitened Lip Areas 140

Summary.. 145

■Chapter 12: The Coloring Book of Digital Painting: Sketching..... 147

A Painter Sketch Workflow: Coloring a Cel.......................... 147

Automatic Sketch Painting: Overlay Blending Mode......................148

Painting a Sketch: Painter's Natural Media Brushes 150

Summary... 159

■Chapter 13: The Animation of Digital Painting:
Physics Engines... 161

Paint Stroke Attributes: Algorithm Control.......................... 161

Audio Expression: Your Digital Painting Vocoder 162

Particle Brushes: Animated Digital Paint Brushes 165

Dynamic Speckle Options: Fattening Your Strokes 169

RealBristle: Simulating Natural Media Brushes..........................170

Summary... 172

■Chapter 14: The Customization of Digital Painting:
Brush Design 173

Brush Customization: Learn All Attributes 173

The Pattern Pen: Painting with Seamless Patterns 174

The Eraser Brush: Bleach Colors, Leaving Texture..........................177

The Blenders Brush: Affecting Colors on a Canvas..........................178

The F-X Brushes: Brushing In Special Effects 181

Smart Strokes: Traditional Brushes Using Effects 184

Summary... 186

■Chapter 15: The Automation of Digital Painting:
Programming.. 189

Content Delivery Programming Platforms 189

Java 7, 8, 9 and JavaFX: A javafx.scene.effect API 190

HTML5 and CSS3: Digital Painting Compositing 192

Android Studio: Java's PorterDuff Blending Modes 193

Game Design: SVG for Collision Detection 195

Painter 2016 Scripting: Coding for Painter 198

Summary 201

■Chapter 16: Publishing Digital Painting:
Content Delivery Platforms... 203

Open Source Formats: PDF, HTML, EPUB.. 203

Portable Document Format: Digital Illustration PDF 204

Hypertext Markup Language: HTML Digital Painting 204

Electronic Publishing: Digital Painting in EPUB3 205

Open Platforms: Java, Android, and Kindle... 205

eBook Readers: Kindle Fire, Android, Java or PDF 205

iTV Sets: Android TV, Java, JavaScript, and HTML5 206

Smartwatches: Android WEAR, Java, and HTML5 206

Smartphone and Tablet: Android, Java, and HTML5 207

Game Console: Android, Java, JavaFX, and HTML5 208

Future Devices: Robots, VR, and Home Appliances.. 208

Paid Software Platforms: iOS or Windows... 209

Apple iPhone and iPad: Supported Media Formats 209

Windows Phone: Supported Digital Media Formats.. 209

Summary 210

Index 211

About the Author

Wallace Jackson has been writing for several leading multimedia publications about work in the new media content development industry, after contributing a piece about advanced-computer-processing architectures for the centerfold (a removable "mini issue" insert) of an original issue of *AV Video Multimedia Producer* magazine *that was* distributed at the SIGGRAPH trade show. Wallace has written for a large number of popular publications about his work in interactive-3D and new-media-advertising campaign design, including: *3DArtist* magazine, *Desktop Publisher Journal*, *CrossMedia* magazine, *Kiosk* magazine, *AV Video Multimedia Producer* magazine, *Digital Signage* magazine, and many other publications.

Wallace Jackson has authored more than a dozen Apress book titles, including four titles in its popular Pro Android series, Java and JavaFX game development titles, digital image compositing titles, digital audio editing titles, digital video editing titles, digital illustration titles, and Android new media content production titles.

In the current book on digital painting and compositing, he focuses on the Inkscape and Corel Painter 2016 digital painting and layer compositing software packages, and uses them to demonstrate digital painting as well as digital image editing and compositing fundamentals to beginners who wish to become digital painting professionals.

Wallace is currently the CEO of Mind Taffy Design, a new media advertising agency which specializes in new media content production and digital campaign design and development, located in La Purisima State Park in Northern Santa Barbara County, on the Point Conception Peninsula, halfway between its clientele in Silicon Valley to the north, and Hollywood, "The OC," West LA, and San Diego to the south.

Mind Taffy Design has created open-source, technology-based (HTML5, JavaScript, Java 8, JavaFX 8, and Android 6.0) digital-new-media i3D content deliverables for more than a quarter century, since January of 1991.

The company's clients consist of a significant number of international brand manufacturers, including IBM, Sony, Tyco, Samsung, Dell, Epson, Nokia, TEAC, Sun Microsystems (Oracle), Micron, SGI, KDS USA, EIZO, CTX International, KFC, Nanao USA, Techmedia, EZC, and Mitsubishi Electronics.

Wallace received his undergraduate BA degree in Business Economics from the University of California at Los Angeles, or UCLA, and his graduate degree in MIS/IT Business Information Systems Design and Implementation from University of Southern California in Los Angeles (USC).

Wallace also received post-graduate degrees from USC, in Entrepreneurship and Marketing Strategy, and completed the USC Graduate Entrepreneurship Program. Wallace earned his two USC degrees while at USC's night-time Marshall School of Business MBA Program, which allowed him to work full-time as a COBOL and RPG-II programmer while completing his business and IT degrees.

You can visit Wallace's blog at `www.wallacejackson.com` to view his multimedia production content. You can also follow him on Twitter at `@wallacejackson`.

About the Technical Reviewer

Chád ("Shod") Darby is an author, instructor, and speaker in the Java development world. As a recognized authority on Java applications and architectures, he has presented technical sessions at software development conferences worldwide (in the United States, UK, India, Russia, and Australia). In his fifteen years as a professional software architect, he's had the opportunity to work for Blue Cross/Blue Shield, Merck, Boeing, Red Hat, and a handful of start-up companies.

Chád is a contributing author to several Java books, including *Professional Java E-Commerce* (Wrox Press), *Beginning Java Networking* (Wrox Press), and *XML and Web Services Unleashed* (Sams Publishing). Chád has Java certifications from Sun Microsystems and IBM. He holds a BS in computer science from Carnegie Mellon University.

You can visit Chád's blog at www.luv2code.com to view his free video tutorials on Java. You can also follow him on Twitter at @darbyluvs2code.

Acknowledgments

I would like to acknowledge all my fantastic editors and their support staff at Apress, who worked those long hours and toiled so very hard on this book, to make it the best digital painting and compositing technique book title currently on the market.

I thank:

Steve Anglin for his work as the Acquisitions Editor for the book and for recruiting me to write development titles at Apress covering widely popular open source content-development platforms (Android, Java, JavaFX, HTML5, CSS3, JS, GIMP, etc.).

Matthew Moodie for his work as the Development Editor on the book and for his experience and guidance during the process of making the book one of the leading image compositing titles.

Mark Powers for his work as the Coordinating Editor for the book and for his constant diligence in making sure that I either hit my chapter delivery deadlines or far surpassed them.

Karen Jameson for her work as the Copy Editor on this book, for her careful attention to minute details, and for ensuring the text conforms to current Apress book writing standards.

Chád Darby for his work as the Technical Reviewer on the book and for making sure that I didn't make technical mistakes.

Introduction

Digital Painting Techniques is intended for the digital artist, digital photographer, multimedia producer, illustrator, application developer, website developer, user interface design architect, user experience designer, social media user, image compositor and just about anyone who's interested in generating high-quality digital paintings or special effects, delivered in popular PNG, JPEG, GIF, BMP, WebP, PSD, and RIFF data formats.

The book covers digital painting, editing and compositing and this equates to digital imaging, digital illustration, and digital painting fundamentals all combined together in one book including technical terms, topics, concepts, and definitions.

Each chapter will build upon the knowledge learned in the previous chapter; thus, later chapters in the book have readers creating advanced digital painting compositing pipelines, using alpha channels, masking, selection sets, blending mode, special effects, editing layers and similar advanced compositing tools.

There is even coverage at the end of this book, regarding data footprint optimization, as well as creating digital image compositing pipelines using open source platforms such as Java, JavaFX, HTML5, CSS3, JavaScript, Scripting, and Android Studio.

In Chapter 1 we install the open source Inkscape software as well as Corel Painter 2016, and take a cursory tour of their user interface designs. In Chapter 2, we learn the foundational information behind both raster imaging and vector illustration, because digital painting is a fusion between these technologies as paint strokes are vector paths while the paint itself is the raster pixels that make up the resulting digital painting image that you see on the display screen.

Chapter 3 introduces you to the Brush, and to your Canvas (Painter) and your Page (Inkscape) drawing surfaces, as well as how to get Painter to create the digital painting automatically for you, by using the Corel Painter 2016 Auto-Paint features.

Chapter 4 covers digital painting or digital illustration concepts of seamlessly tileable patterns (Inkscape), as well as weaves (Painter) and gradients. Vector concepts of stroking and filling vector shapes is also covered during this chapter.

Chapter 5 covers the plethora of hardware products which make professional digital painting possible, including stand-alone stylus products, tablet+stylus products, and touchscreen-display-enabled tablet+stylus products. You can still use your mouse with this book; however, if you don't yet have a digital painting hardware set-up, as all of the examples for this book are designed to be mouse-friendly so all users can play along.

Chapter 6 covers digital painting "nozzles" in Painter to use with the Image Hose Brush category. Not only do we use the Image Hose with Nozzles, to blow imagery all over your Canvas, but we also learn how to create your own professional Nozzles, using any images that you want to use in your digital painting!

Chapter 7 covers Painter 2016's Quick Clone feature. This allows you to use your digital photograph as a source image and apply your own digital paint brush strokes, which use the color from the source image, to create a digital painting out of your favorite digital photography assets.

Chapter8 covers SVG Plug-In Filters in Inkscape and Plug In Effects in Painter. These apply algorithmic special effects to your digital illustrations, digital paintings, and digital imagery, and are not only available in Inkscape but in HTML5.

Chapter 9 starts to get into more advanced concepts, like selection sets, pulling masks, and storing the mask using alpha channels. We look at a Painter 2016 magic wand tool, and how to select objects within your compositions, as well as how you can select your vector objects in Inkscape.

Chapter 10 discusses layers, and the layer-based approach that digital compositing software packages, including imaging, illustration, video, painting and even audio, take to create a complex new media asset. This chapter also covers algorithmic, Porter-Duff "blending modes," called "composite methods" within Painter, and called the blend mode within Inkscape.

Chapter 11 covers how to do photo-retouching with Painter 2016 tools. This shows how similar Painter 2016 is to popular image editing software, and shows how to prepare your digital photographs for a cloning process that turns them into artwork.

Chapter 12 shows the Painter "Sketch and Paint" workflow, including the sketch algorithm, and how to use layers and masks (selection sets) to utilize this workflow. This builds upon the previous two chapters' content.

Chapter 13 covers Algorithmic Brushing Engines in Painter including physical systems, fluid dynamics, natural media brush simulation, and similar brushes where algorithms do most of the work in creating the effect that the brush has on the paper you have selected to use to capture the brush strokes and dynamics.

Chapter 14 covers Brush Design and Brush Categories using Brush Variants to explore how the hundreds of Brush Parameters will allow you to create your own custom digital paintbrushes.

Chapter 15 covers Scripts in Painter, as well as computer programming languages and how they factor into digital painting and layer compositing. I cover most of your popular open source platforms, such as Java 8, JavaFX, Android 6, Kindle and HTML5.

Chapter 16 covers publishing digital painting artwork for leading content delivery platforms and popular hardware devices spanning from smartwatches to UHD 4K iTV interactive television sets and everything in between, including e-Readers, HD tablets and smartphones.

If you are interested in digital painting and you want to learn the fundamentals, and how everything works, in the digital painting domain from algorithmic brush dynamics to creating the multi-layer compositing pipeline, this is the digital painting and special effects book for you.

The book is overflowing with tips, tricks, tools, topics, terminology, techniques, concepts, and work processes. Indeed, this Digital Painting Techniques book can give you the boost to transition from digital painting neophyte to that knowledgeable professional that you seek to become, at least where a digital painting and digital layer compositing pipeline is concerned.

■ ■ ■

CHAPTER 1

Digital Painting Software: Corel Painter and Inkscape

Welcome to *Digital Painting Techniques*! This book will take you through the terminology, concepts, and techniques involved in digital painting. Digital painting is a fusion of the popular digital image compositing and digital illustration new media genres, with a sprinkle of physics algorithms and special effects thrown in for good measure. We will also cover technical issues such as codecs and formats, how to use digital painting assets with popular computer programming languages, and open source content publishing platforms such as Kindle, Android Studio, HTML5, and JavaFX, and similar issues allowing you to "bridge" your digital artwork with interactive new media creations.

I will start with low-level concepts: in this chapter it is the **software tools**, and how to download and install them for use during this book. After that, we'll build upon foundational concepts from each previous chapter in the subsequent chapters, until you get a comprehensive understanding of digital painting and all the complex subjects and components that factor into it such as raster data, vector data, RGB colors, alpha, gradients, patterns, brushes, nozzles, dynamics, physics, tablet or stylus hardware, multilayer compositing, image formats, work process, physics algorithms, special effects processing, data footprint optimization, open source computer programming, and interactive content publishing.

I will show you how these concepts, techniques, and terms apply to Corel Painter and the Inkscape open source digital illustration software package. This just so happens to be free for commercial use and very similar in features to Adobe Illustrator and CorelDRAW.

For this reason part of the chapter, logically the first part, would be how to download and install open source Inkscape software, just in case you do not have any digital painting and illustration software on your multimedia workstation currently. Then, you'll learn about the foundational elements of digital illustration.

All our readers are going to need to have digital illustration software of one type or another, whether that is **Corel Painter** or the open source (free) Inkscape. If you do not own Corel Painter, you can use the free for commercial use **Inkscape.** Corel Painter also has a trial version you can use during this book.

Downloading and Installing Inkscape

Let's install Inkscape first on Windows, Mac OS X, or Linux.

Inkscape.org: Get Inkscape Illustration Software

To download the current stable version of Inkscape, you will go to:
http://www.inkscape.org, and click on the green **Download Arrow** link seen in
Figure 1-1; or alternately click the **Download** tab, directly underneath and to the right of
the **Draw Freely** slogan.

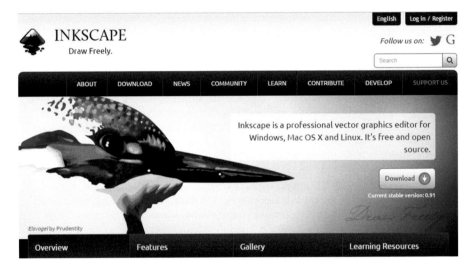

Figure 1-1. *Go to the inkscape.org and click the Download arrow*

Download the **inkscape-0.91-x64.msi** installer file if you are using Windows, or a
Linux or Mac version. Next, right-click on it and select the **Install** option to start your
installation process. Inkscape for Windows uses a 64-bit version, since most modern-day
workstations run 64-bit Windows Vista, 7, 8.1, or 10. Figure 1-2 shows the downloaded
file, which has been selected, and right-clicked on to reveal the context-sensitive menu,
with this **Install** option selected in blue. If for some reason you do not own a 64-bit
content production workstation, go to Walmart and get one for under $600.

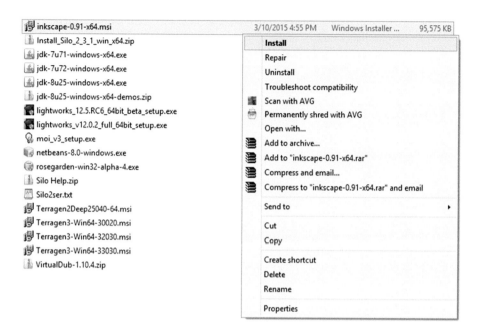

Figure 1-2. *Right-click on .MSI file, and select Install option*

You can purchase a brand name workstation tower for $450 to $600 at Walmart, or on http://www.PriceWatch.com. I've used, and recommend, the Acer, HP, Dell, Razer, and Compaq workstations.

Once your installation starts, click the **Next** button, as is shown on the left-hand side of Figure 1-3.

Figure 1-3. *Click Next, then Next, then the Typical Button*

Once you click on the **Next** button you'll get an **End-User License Agreement** dialog. Select the "I accept the terms in the License Agreement" check box and then click on **Next** to continue.

Next, click on a **Typical** installation type button, as is seen on the right-hand side in Figure 1-3, to specify a default installation, which will include everything that you will need.

This will give you the **Ready to Install Inkscape** dialog, seen in Figure 1-4 on the left, where you can click on **Install**.

Figure 1-4. *Click the Install Button to begin the installation*

You will then get your **Installing Inkscape** progress bar, and once that has finished, the **Completed Inkscape Setup Wizard** dialog will appear. Click the **Finish** button, and install shortcut icons to Inkscape on the desktop or taskbar for easy launch access. Once you have done this, launch Inkscape, and make sure that it works. You should see what is shown in Figure 1-5. Once you have Inkscape installed, we can move on and install Painter.

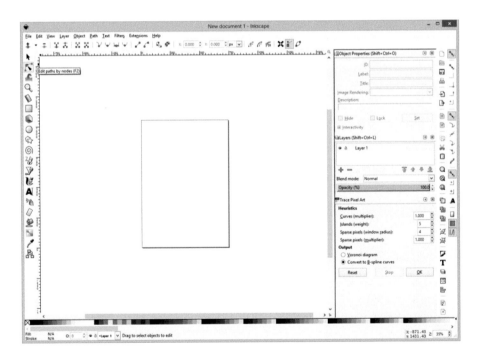

Figure 1-5. *Launch Inkscape to make sure it installed correctly*

Corel Painter 2016: Installing the Software

Next, let's install Corel Painter 2016, which you can get from Corel at a discount, if you've purchased this book, so the book ends up being an amazing investment! You can also use the free trial version as you go through this book, so you don't have to make that investment until you have learned more about this digital painting software package. This is one software package you will want to add to your content production workstation and pipeline. First you will download the **Painter 2016 x64.exe** file from http://www.PainterArtist.com, and then run the installer from your browser downloads area by selecting **Run** this file, or right-clicking the EXE file and selecting **Run as Administrator**. This launches the Installer Wizard dialog, seen in Figure 1-6.

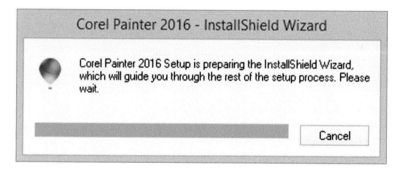

Figure 1-6. *Launch the Corel Painter 2016 InstallShield Wizard*

As you can see in Figure 1-7 once you accept the default installation location folder of: C:/Program Files/Corel/Painter2016, you will get a progress bar dialog showing you the installation as it progresses through the stages of software installation.

Figure 1-7. *Install to /Program Files/Corel/Painter2016 folder*

Once your installation has completed, you will get this Installation Wizard has been successful dialog, where you will want to select your **Check for product updates** option, as shown in Figure 1-8. This will make certain that you have the latest Painter files on your new media content production workstation.

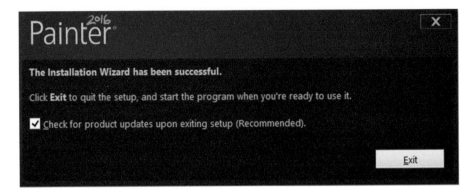

Figure 1-8. *Check for product updates upon exiting setup dialog*

Once you click on this **Exit** button, you'll then get your Painter 2016 **Checking for Updates** dialog, as shown on your left side of Figure 1-9. For my Particular installation, since I have just downloaded this Painter 2016 software, this came up with a **There are no updates available at this time** dialog.

Figure 1-9. *Checking for updates dialog; click OK when updated*

Setting Up Painter 2016: Adding Painter in Taskbar

After you click on the OK button, you can open up the OS file management utility and find your Painter executable file. Once you find the Painter executable file, you will then right-click on this executable, and use a Pin to Taskbar option to create the Quick Launch Icon for your desktop.

This can be seen on the right side of Figure 1-10 in the right-click context-sensitive menu, where you can select **Pin to Start** (Menu) or **Pin to Taskbar**, or you can pin Painter to both.

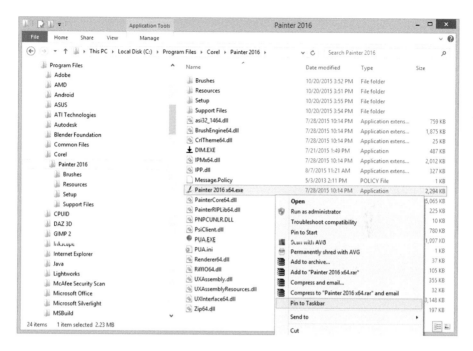

Figure 1-10. *Find Painter2016x64.exe and right-click and select Pin to Taskbar*

Once you have a Quick Launch Icon, you can then click on it anytime, to launch Painter 2016. Let's do that now. You will get a Painter 2016 startup screen, as is shown in Figure 1-11, while the software loads into your workstation's system memory.

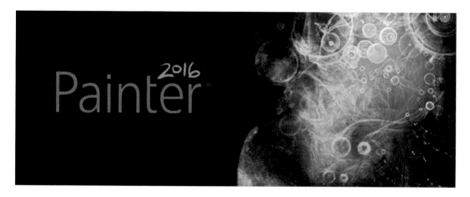

Figure 1-11. *Click the QuickLaunch Icon in TaskBar to launch Corel Painter 2016*

7

Once Painter 2016 launches you will get a control panel, shown in Figure 1-12, where you can learn Painter 2016, and get content, or even get inspired by other digital painting artists if you like. This will always come up on Painter 2016 launch as long as you leave your **Show this at startup** checkbox selected.

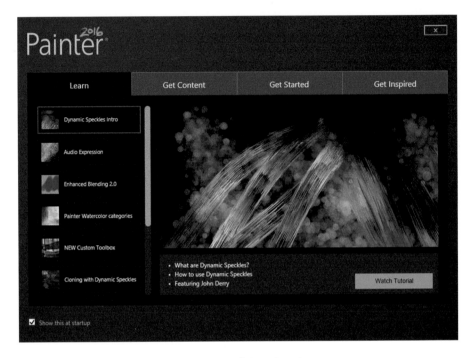

Figure 1-12. *The Painter 2016 Startup Screen's User Interface*

I like to leave the Show this at startup option selected so that I always have this Painter 2016 control panel available to me, in case that I ever need it later on for any of the four different areas of interest that it offers Painter 2016 users.

If you do not select anything inside the startup control panel, a time-out will eventually bring up the **New Image** dialog automatically, so that you can create a new image to work on.

I named my document Digital_Painting_CH1, as you can see in Figure 1-13, and then I accepted these default settings for the new image dialog.

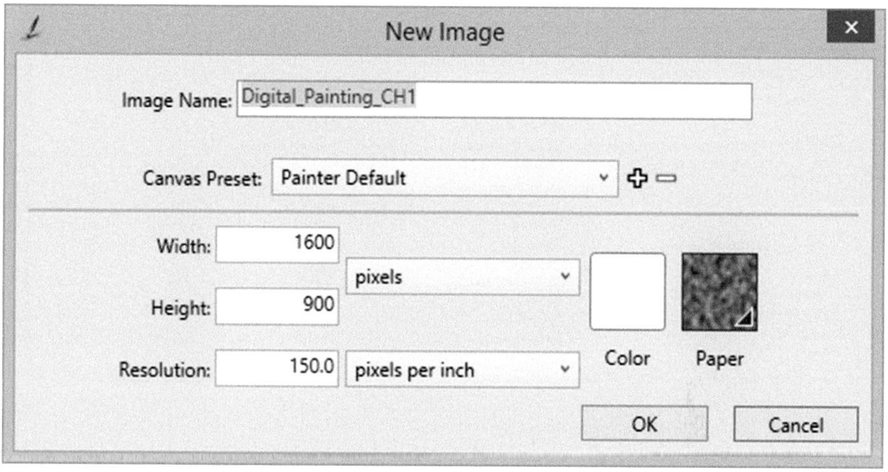

Figure 1-13. A New Image dialog shows after Startup times out

The default resolution uses a 16:9 HDTV aspect ratio, at 1600 by 900 pixels, which is a common laptop resolution for the laptops that have 17.3" displays, which is most of them, these days. At 150 PPI (Pixels Per Inch) or DPI (Dots Per Inch), this equates to 10.67" (1600/150) wide, and 6" (900/150) tall.

Next, let's take a look at how to install Painter Brush Packs, which allow you to add powerful tools to Painter 2016.

Enhancing Painter 2016: Installing Brush Packs

Corel offers something called Painter Brush Packs so you can enhance your Painter 2016 installation with some additional physics-based brush settings. We will take a closer look at how to create your own custom brushes during this book. The Painter Team has spent a lot of time creating the Brush Pack collection of custom brushes, which can save you valuable time, and allows you to get right down to creating digital painting artwork. You don't need to purchase Brush Packs to do the exercises for this book, so don't worry about purchasing all of these Brush Packs. That said, these Brush Packs are fantastic tools for expanding your creative quiver and for giving you more artistic options.

If you purchased and downloaded any of these Corel Brush Packs, you probably downloaded them to the same folder location as the `Painter2016x64.exe` file. In my case this was a `C:/Painter2016` folder, which is shown on the left side of Figure 1-14.

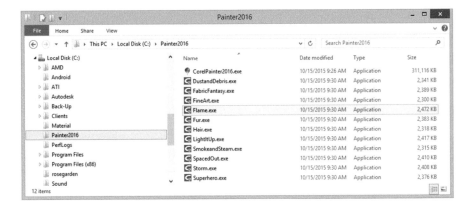

Figure 1-14. *Install your custom brushes*

As you can see I downloaded 11 of the Corel Brush Packs, allowing me to enhance Painter 2016 with powerful physics-based brush engines to enhance my creativity by an order of magnitude allowing me to get to the actual client project workflow rather than building the digital painting brush tools that I will need to create those client deliverables.

Next, let's install one of these Brush Packs, to see how they all would be installed. Double-click on your DustandDebris installer EXE, or any of the Brush Packs that you have decided to purchase and download, and launch the installation process.

Your first dialog will be an Extracting dialog, shown on the left side in Figure 1-15. Next, you should get the License Agreement dialog, where you need to accept a license agreement.

Figure 1-15. *Launch Installer Wizard, and accept the agreement*

After you click on the **Install** button, which is shown in the middle of Figure 10-10, you will get an **Installing** progress bar dialog, shown on the right side of Figure 10-10.

Next, launch Painter and make sure that it's working, as you did with Inkscape in the previous section of the chapter. I will take a closer look at the primary areas for Painter's user interface, and for Inkscape, in the next chapter of this book.

Summary

In this first chapter I made sure that you had digital painting software packages installed and ready to master. You installed the open source Inkscape and professional Corel Painter 2016 software, which you will be using over the course of this book to explore a plethora of digital painting techniques.

In Chapter 2 you will take a closer look at the user interface for both Inkscape as well as Corel Painter 2016.

CHAPTER 2

■ ■ ■

The Terminology of Digital Painting: Vector and Raster

Now that you have the digital illustration and digital painting software packages installed, it's time to get into underlying concepts that span digital illustration and digital painting. Digital imaging software, such as GIMP, Photoshop, and PaintShop Pro are based on "raster" or pixel-based technologies. I wrote a book called *Digital Image Compositing Fundamentals* (Apress, 2015) if you want to dive into **raster imaging** in detail. There is also a "vector" or math-based technology that is used in digital illustration and 3D software packages such as Inkscape or Blender. I wrote a *Digital Illustration Fundamentals* (Apress, 2015) book, covering this area, if you want to dive into **vector illustration** in further detail as well.

I will start with low-level concepts; in this chapter it is the **raster image** and **vector illustration** and how they differ from each other. We'll look at the foundational concepts behind raster images and vector illustration, and see how the software that you installed in Chapter 1 bridges these two technologies, using features such as patterns, brushes, weaves, and nozzles.

After that we will take a look at primary user interface areas, including canvas, menus, toolbars, floating palettes, and tabs for both your Inkscape and Painter 2016 software packages.

Computer Graphics: Raster versus Vector

Digital Computer Graphics come in two flavors: **raster** or **vector** unless you are using digital painting software or 3D software, in which case you will be using a seamless blending of the two. In this chapter, we'll cover the technical basics of vector and raster, as well as how digital painting or 3D software uses both of these together to create visually exciting artwork. Even the digital illustration packages use some raster elements to allow them to add some visual wow factor, by using **seamless patterns**.

Basic Vector Shapes: Vertices, Lines, and Curves

Digital illustration vector images are composed of shape object constructs. These are composed of **data points**, called **vertices**, or, in Inkscape, nodes. These are placed in 2D space using **X,Y coordinates**. Lines, arcs, or curves will then connect the **vertex** points together. We will be looking at concepts and terminology for these points, lines, and curves during this section. If you create **closed shapes**, that is, one where there are no openings, for a **fill** (color, pattern, or gradient) to escape, you can also fill a vector shape, so that the shape looks solid instead of empty. In fact you can fill an open shape, but the fill will act as though the shape was closed, so this isn't usually done.

The Vertex: A Foundation for 2D and 3D Geometry

The foundation for any 2D (or any 3D) vector **geometry** asset is called the **vertex**. Multiple **vertices** (the plural of vertex) are required to create a **line** or **arc**, which require two vertices, or a **closed shape**, which requires at least two vertices, if you are using Bézier curves, or three vertices if you are using straight lines. Vertices are used in vector SVG data processing as well as in 3D OpenGL vector data processing, both of which are integrated into Java, JavaFX, HTML5, and in Android Studio.

Vertex data is outlined in SVG using X,Y coordinates, as mentioned earlier, which tell the processor where the vertex is located in 2D space. Without these vertex coordinates lines and curves cannot be drawn, as they must have an **origin**, as well as a **destination** vertex coordinate, as part of vector line drawing operations. A line or arc would be an example of an **open shape**.

If you look into creating or programming **SVG data** you'll notice that these X,Y numeric pairs are the majority of the SVG data, which can be contained using the **XML format**, or in a **Java SVG object** for Android Studio application. SVG data can also be used in your **JavaScript** (HTML5) code as well as in **JavaFX** (Java 8 or Java 9) code, so it is compatible across each of your open platform new media application or content development workflow.

An X,Y coordinate, all by its lonesome, is what's termed **one dimensional** or **1D**. You'll need two vertex coordinates to be considered to be two dimensional, or 2D, so, a line or a curve, that is, an open shape, or a closed shape, will be a 2D object.

Next, let's take a look at the next level up from the 1D vertex shape element, the 2D **path** vector shape element. This 2D path data comprises the majority of a **scalable vector graphics**, or SVG, shape definition, which can be defined using XML, Java, JavaFX, Android Studio, HTML5, or JavaScript.

The Path: Connect the Vertices to Create a Shape

Your path is defined in SVG using a "path data" element. Both an open shape, as well as a closed shape, are technically paths, according to the open source SVG specification. This SVG Path represents the outline of an open or closed shape that can be **filled**, **stroked**, or even used as a **clipping** path. We will be covering these concepts in detail during the book, but briefly, a fill deals with the interior of a path; strokes deal with the line or curve thickness that styles your path; and the clipping path is used for Boolean operations, or cutting interiors out.

In SVG data an SVG Path object represents 2D "geometry," used to outline a Path object. In fact, in JavaFX, the class is actually called the **SVGPath** class. SVG path data can be defined in terms of **SVG commands**. Briefly, some of the commands include a **moveto** command, which sets a current point; a **lineto** command, which draws a straight line; and a **curveto** command, which draws a cubic Bézier curve. A **closepath** command will be used to close an open shape, drawing a closing line to the shape start point.

Compound paths are also possible in SVG; these allow you to create complex, Boolean shape special effects. For instance, you could use a compound path to create a hole in your shape.

Vector support is included in digital painting software, such as Painter 2016, to allow digital illustrations within the software, as well as to base more complex brush strokes, on top of these vector paths. This is necessary to base advanced brush strokes on top of, as well as adding physics (dynamics) to your brush stroke. Brush stroke dynamics will be easier to implement using vector paths, than raster pixel arrays, which you will be learning about in the next section of this chapter.

Corel has another software package called CorelDRAW that also bridges vector illustration and raster imaging together. I remember this software from decades ago, so an artistic concept of using vector illustration technology and raster imaging in a unified digital artisan environment is nothing new.

Another genre of software that uses vector technologies as the foundation with raster imagery on top of it is called 3D (or interactive 3D, or i3D) software. Blender is an open source 3D (and i3D) software package if you're interested in exploring this complex new media genre.

So, digital painting is a fusion of vector stroke paths, with raster paint effects applied on top of them, which is why we are covering vector concepts first in this chapter, as they provide the foundation for your brush strokes; where they **start** and **end**, if they are **straight** or **curved**; and **4D** considerations, such as stroke **speed**. There are also radial math considerations such as the **angle** (vertical to laying down) or **rotation** of your stylus around a 360 circle around the perimeter of your stylus.

Raster Concepts: Pixels, Aspect Ratio, Color, and Alpha

The raster approach to imaging is completely different from the vector approach. Whereas a vector approach uses math to define imagery using illustrations created by SVG commands, the raster approach uses tiny dots to create an image when you look at the dots all at once, not close up, but from a distance, like with those signs in Las Vegas where you can't see what is on them when you are right in front of them but see a brilliant image when you are the right distance away from them.

Picture Elements: Pixels Are Your Raster Image Building Blocks

Digital Images are made up of two-dimensional, or 2D, arrays (or grids) containing something called "pixels." This industry term **pixel** is the combination of two terms: **pictures** (hip folks call these "pix") and **elements** (shortened to be just els). Thus the foundation for any digital image that you will be working with is its picture elements. These pixels dictate everything about your digital image asset, such as its file size, dimension, color, transparency, and shape. It is important to note that digital illustration assets aren't made up of pixels, at least not until the SVG commands that compose them are converted to pixels by using an algorithmic process called "rendering."

Image Resolution: The Number of Pixels in Your Raster Image

The number of pixels contained in a digital image asset is expressed using a term called **resolution**. This is the number of pixels contained in the image. Images have a width, which is usually denoted using a W; or alternatively, using an X, which stands for your x-axis; as well as the height, which is denoted using an H; or using a Y for the y-axis. Image resolution gives you a digital image's 2D **dimensions**. For instance a popular VGA resolution is expressed by specifying **800x600**. Alternately, you could also use the word "by," for instance, **800 by 600** pixels.

To find the total number of pixels that are contained in any 2D digital image, you will want to **multiply** width pixels by height pixels, or, in coding terms **Resolution = Width * Height**.

Hopefully, you remember the **area of a rectangle** equation from grade school. Here it is again in the professional digital painting application context. As an example, an **HDTV** resolution **1920x1080** image will contain **2,073,600** pixels if you multiplied the width and height together. If you like digital photography, you're probably familiar with the term two **megapixels**, which is referring to 2.00 million pixels. This is essentially what this HDTV resolution is giving you in terms of the number of pixels.

The more pixels that are contained in the digital image, the higher its resolution will be said to be. Higher resolution images will give the viewer more **detail** or image subject matter **definition**. This is why **HDTV** is called **High Definition**, and why the new 4K resolution **UHD** TVs are called Ultra High **Definition**.

Image Aspect Ratio: The 2D Ratio of W:H Pixels in Your Image

Closely related to the number of pixels in your digital image is the ratio of X to Y pixels in a digital image. This is called the **aspect ratio**. This concept of aspect ratio is more complicated than the image resolution, because it is the **ratio** of width to height, or **W:H**, within image resolution dimensions. If you like to think in terms of an image x-axis and y-axis, it would be **X:Y**. This aspect ratio defines a shape for your image, and this concept also applies to the shape of a display screen. For instance, a smartwatch will have a square aspect (1:1), and a widescreen iTV Set will have a wide rectangular aspect (2:1).

A 1:1 aspect ratio digital image (or display screen) can be said to be perfectly square. Since this is the aspect ratio, by its very definition, a 1:1 aspect ratio is the same as a 2:2 or a 3:3 aspect ratio image. It is important to note that it is this ratio between these two numbers that defines the shape of the image or screen, not the numbers themselves, and that's why it is called an aspect ratio, although it's often called aspect for short. A 2:1 aspect ratio would create a widescreen aspect.

Your image aspect ratio is generally expressed using the smallest set or pair of numbers that can be achieved (reduced) on either side of the aspect ratio colon. If you paid attention in high school, when you were all learning about the lowest (or least) common denominator, then aspect ratio mathematics should be fairly easy for you to calculate.

I would do this mathematical matriculation by continuing to divide each side by two. Let's take a fairly weird 1280x1024 (termed SXGA) resolution as an example.

Half of 1280:1024 is 640:512, half of 640:512 would then be 320:256. Half of that is 160:128, and half of that is 80:64. Half of that is 40:32, and half of that is 20:16. Half of that is 10:8, and half of that is 5:4. Therefore, an SXGA resolution uses a 5:4 aspect ratio.

Interestingly, all the above ratios were the same aspect ratio, and all were valid. Thus, if you want to take the really easy way out, replace that "x" in your image resolution, with a colon, and you have an aspect ratio for the image. The industry standard involves distilling an aspect ratio down to its lowest format, as we've done here, as that is a far more useful ratio.

Next let's take a look at how a pixel defines its color.

RGB Color Theory: Each Pixel Contains Three Color Channels

Within the array of pixels that makes up your resolution and its aspect ratio, each of your pixels will be holding color values, using three **color channels**, in something called the **RGB color space**. RGB stands for the Red, Green, and Blue pixel color values each pixel can define that establishes what color it is.

Color channels were originally used in the digital image compositing programs like GIMP, for compositing digital imagery for use on display screens, or to be printed out using inks, on printers, which use a different color space called **CMYK**.

Color channels are sometimes referred to as **color plates** in the printing industry, due to older printing presses, which used metal plates – some of which are still in use today.

In GIMP, color channels have their own **Channels** palette, and allow us to work on just that color channel (or plate), as can be quite useful for special effects or other advanced image operations. Painter 2016 also has a Channels palette.

An opposite of **additive** color (RGB) is **subtractive** color (CMYK), which is used in printing, and involves using inks. Inks subtract color from each other, rather than adding color, which is what happens when you combine colors by using light.

Using Red and Green as an example, using additive color, Red+Green=Yellow. Using subtractive color, Red+Green=Purple, so as you can see, additive gives you brighter color (adds light), while subtractive gives you darker color (i.e., subtracts light).

To create millions of different color values using these RGB color channels, what you will need to do is vary the levels or intensities for each of the individual RGB color values. The amount, or numbers, of red, green, and blue values or levels of intensity of light that you have available to mix together will determine the total number of colors that you would be able to reproduce. Color needs to be generated for every image pixel.

Every pixel in an image will contain **256 levels** of color intensity for each of the RGB (red, green, and blue) color data values. **Color intensity** (or brightness) data inside each of the digital image pixels is represented with a brightness level for each color. This can range between zero (brightness turned off) and 255 (brightness fully on), and controls the amount of color contributed by each pixel for each of these red, green, and blue colors in your digital image.

To calculate a total amount of available colors is easy, as it is again simple **multiplication**. If you multiply 256 times 256 times 256 you get **16,777,216** colors. This represents unique color combinations of Red, Green, and Blue, which you can obtain using these 256 levels (data values) per color that you have to work with across these three different additive color channels.

Pixel Color Depth: Bit-Levels That Define the Number of Colors

The amount of color available to each pixel in a digital image is referred to in the industry as the **color depth** for an image. Common color depths used in digital image assets include 8-bit, 16-bit, 24-bit, 32-bit, 48-bit, and 64-bit.

The **true color** depth image will feature the 24-bit color depth and will thus contain 16,777,216 colors. High color depth images feature 16-bit color depth.

File formats that support both 16-bit and 24-bit color depth include the BMP, XCF, PSD, TGA, and TIFF. True color only image formats include JPEG (or JPG), PNG, and WebP.

Using true color depth will give you the highest quality level. This is why I'm recommending the use of PNG24, or PNG32, for your digital painting. Next let's take a look indexed color values in case you're optimizing your imagery for the Internet.

Indexed Color Depth: Using Palettes to Hold 256 Colors

The lowest color depth exists in 8-bit **indexed color** images. These feature a maximum of 256 color values, which is why they are 8-bit images, and use an indexed "palette" of colors, which is why they are called indexed color images. Popular image file formats for indexed color include GIF, PNG, TIFF, BMP, or Targa. The indexed color palette is created by the indexed color **codec** when you "export" your file from an imaging software package, such as GIMP. Codec stands for **CO**de-**DEC**ode and is an algorithm that can optimize a file size to be smaller using **compression**.

The way you convert 24-bit, truecolor image data to this indexed color image format (GIF, PNG8) with Photoshop is to use the **File ➤ Save for Web** menu sequence. This will open your Save for Web dialog, which will allow you to set a file format (GIF, or PNG), number of colors (from 2, up to 256), color conversion algorithm (perceptual, selective, adaptive or restrictive), the dithering algorithm (diffusion, pattern or noise), and a number of other advanced options, such as progressive interlacing. I'd recommend using Perceptual color conversion, 256 colors, and a diffusion dither algorithm for the best visual results.

To convert truecolor image data into indexed color image data using GIMP 2.8.14, you use the **Image ➤ Mode ➤ Indexed** menu sequence. This will call up an Indexed Color Conversion dialog. This has fewer options than your Photoshop Save for Web dialog, but the important ones are there so you can specify color depth and diffusion dithering. I recommend using GIMP Floyd-Steinberg diffusion dithering algorithm. There is even an algorithm that reduces color bleeding, keeping image edges clean and sharp.

As an example of color depth, if you selected 2 colors that would be a 1-bit (PNG1) image, 4 colors would be a PNG2 (2-bit color depth) image, 16 colors would be a 4-bit PNG4 color depth image, 64 colors would be a 6-bit PNG6, and 128 colors would be a 7-bit PNG7 image.

Next, let's take a look at the other color format 24-bit truecolor, or 32-bit truecolor plus alpha channel transparency.

True Color Depth: Using 24-bit True Color Imagery

One of the most widely used digital image file formats in the world is the **JPEG** file format, and it only comes in one flavor: 24-bit color. Other file formats which support 24-bits of color data include Windows BMP, TIFF, Targa (TGA), Photoshop (PSD), and PNG24. Since the PNG format supports 8-bit (PNG8) or 32-bit (PNG32) color, I call a 24-bit PNG format PNG24, to be precise. The primary difference in the truecolor file formats comes down to a format characteristic: **lossy** versus **lossless** compression.

Lossy compression means that an algorithm, which is also called a codec (COde-DECode), is throwing away some of the data to achieve a smaller data footprint. For this reason, save your original uncompressed file format using a lossless data format, prior to applying any lossy compression, in this case, JPEG.

Lossless compression, used by the PNG, BMP, TGA, and TIFF formats, doesn't throw away any original image data; it applies an algorithm that finds **patterns** that result in less data used, and that can 100% reconstruct all of the original pixel color values.

True color images are used for user interface design, or for web sites and application content. They can also be used for other digital content, which is displayed using eBooks, iTV Set Apps, Games, Smartwatch faces, Digital Signage, and social media sharing forums that support digital imagery and illustration.

Using more than one image for digital painting is called **image (layer) compositing**. Compositing involves using more than one single image layer. The background, or **backplate** image uses 24-bit image data. All your other layers in a compositing stack above a background plate need to support **transparency**, and you will need to use **32-bits** of data, which is known as **ARGB** or as **RGBA**.

This transparency is provided by a fourth channel, known as your **alpha channel**. I'm going to introduce you to this next.

True Color plus Alpha: Using 32-bit Digital Imagery

Besides 8-bit, 16-bit, and 24-bit digital imagery, there is also 32-bit digital imagery. Formats that support the 32-bit color depth include PNG, TIFF, TGA, BMP, and PSD. I like to use **PNG32** as it's supported in HTML, Java, JavaFX, CSS, and Android, where other file formats are not used in open source platforms.

These 32-bits of image data include 24-bits of RGB color data, plus 8-bits of "alpha," or transparency, value data, held in what is commonly referred to as your alpha channel.

Since you now know that 8-bits holds 256 values, it will make sense to you that an alpha channel will hold 256 different levels of transparency data values, for each pixel in a digital image. This is important for digital image compositing, because it allows layers that hold this 32-bit image data to allow some portion (from 0 to 255, or all of that pixel's color) of the color data to bleed through to (or to blend with) layers below.

Next, let's take a close look at what alpha channels do.

Alpha Channels: Defining the Transparency for Each Pixel

Let's take a look at how alpha channels define digital image pixel transparency values, and how they can be utilized to composite digital painting compositions. Alpha channel data provides transparency inside of a digital painting compositing pipeline in software such as Inkscape and Painter 2016. I would term this "static" use, but alpha data can also be used via PNG digital image assets to composite digital imagery in real time, using open platforms such as Android Studio, HTML5, CSS3, Java, and JavaFX. I would term this "dynamic" use, as the code allows you to access the pixel transparency values in a millisecond of time, so you can animate the data in any way that you like: for example. in web sites, games, animated user interface design, iTV programs, interactive eBooks, and smart watch faces.

Digital image compositing involves the seamless blending together of more than one layer of digital imagery, and, as you might imagine, per pixel transparency is an important concept.

Digital image compositing needs to be used when you want to create an image on your display that appears as though it is one single image (or an animation) but is actually the seamless collection of more than one composited image layers. One of the principle reasons you would want to set up image, or animation, composition is to allow you more control over various elements in an image composite by having components on different layers.

To accomplish multilayer compositing, you always need to have an Alpha Channel transparency value, which you can utilize to precisely control the blending of the pixel's color with the pixels in the same X,Y image location on other layers below it.

Like the RGB color channels, the alpha channel will have 256 levels of transparency from 100% transparent (zero) to 100% opaque (255). Each pixel will have different alpha transparency data just like each pixel will have different RGB color values. This is the reason that the Layers and Channels tabs in Painter are grouped together in the same floating palette, as you will see layer on in this chapter, when we look at user interfaces.

Porter and Duff: Your Algorithmic Pixel Blending Modes

There is another powerful aspect of layered compositing, called the **blending modes**. Any of you who are Photoshop or GIMP users have seen that each layer in digital imagery compositing software will be able to be "set" to use one different blending mode. Blending modes are algorithms that specify how the pixels for a layer are blended mathematically with the previous layers underneath that layer.

These pixel blending algorithms will take into account a pixel's transparency level. Between these two image compositing controls, you can achieve virtually any compositing result that you are trying to achieve in Inkscape or in Painter.

A major difference for dynamic platforms such as Android is that blending modes can be controlled **interactively** by using custom Java or JavaFX programming logic. Some of these powerful PorterDuff Java class blending modes include XOR, ADD, SCREEN, OVERLAY, DARKEN, LIGHTEN, and MULTIPLY. The *Pro Android Graphics* (Apress, 2013) title covers how to implement PorterDuff blending modes inside the complex image compositing pipeline, if you are interested in diving into an area of Android in greater detail.

Smoothing Edges in Digital Painting: Anti-aliasing Algorithms

Anti-aliasing is a digital image technique that is also implemented by using an algorithm. What this algorithm does, is it finds where two adjacent colors meet along an edge, blending those pixel colors around that jagged edge. Anti-aliasing will add averaged colors along the edge between two colored areas to visually smooth those two colors together, along the (formerly) jagged edge. This will make a jagged edge appear to be smooth, especially when the image is zoomed out, and the pixels are not individually visible.

What anti-aliasing does is to trick the eyes into seeing smoother edges, eliminating what's commonly called the **jaggies**. Anti-aliasing provides impressive results, using few (usually, fewer than eight) intermediary averaged color values, for those pixels which lie along the edges within the image that need to be made to look smoother.

By averaged color I mean colors or a spectrum of colors, which is part of the way between the two colors that intersect along that edge which is being anti-aliased. I created a visual example of anti-aliasing for you, to show the resulting effect. I first created the seemingly smooth red circle, seen in Figure 2-1, against a yellow background. I zoomed into an edge of that circle, and then I grabbed a screenshot. I placed this next to the zoomed-out circle, to show the orange anti-aliasing pixels.

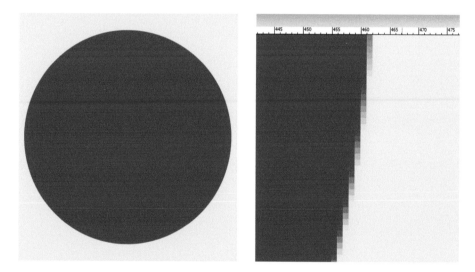

Figure 2-1. *A zoomed-in view (right) shows anti-aliasing effect*

Notice there are 7 or 8 averaged colors that are used to create this visual effect. One of the tricks that I utilize to implement my own anti-aliasing effect is to use a **Gaussian Blur** filter on any jagged edges in digital paintings in Inkscape or in Painter. This will also work in GIMP 2.8 or in Photoshop CS.

Be sure to use **low blur values** (0.2 to 0.4) on a subject (as well as its alpha channel), which has these jagged edges.

This will provide the same anti-aliasing that you see in Figure 2-1, and not only that, it will "blur" the alpha channel transparency values as well.

Blurring the alpha channel will allow your alpha channel to anti-alias a 32-bit image object with any background imagery you may be attempting to seamlessly composite it against. Next, let's take a tour of your Inkscape and Painter user interfaces.

Inkscape: Tour of Primary User Interface

Launch Inkscape using the quick launch icon on the taskbar that you created in Chapter 1. The user interface, as seen in Figure 2-2, has nine primary areas that you need to be concerned with. These include menus, tool options, floating palettes, standard operation icons, snap alignment icons, primary tools, color set swatches, your current tool settings, and your drawing canvas. These are shown, numbered one through nine, in Figure 2-2, and Figure 2-3 shows the other three palettes in Inkscape's docking area (numbered as 3) for Layers, Fill, Strokes, and Properties.

Figure 2-2. *The nine primary Inkscape user interface regions*

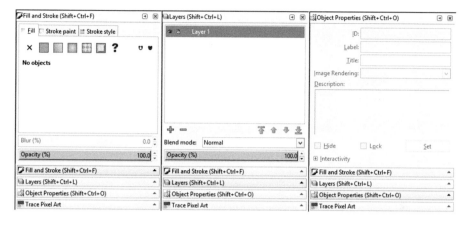

Figure 2-3. *Fill and Stroke, Layers, and Object Properties panes*

Click the collapsed palettes shown in a docking area (#3 in Figure 2-2), to open the three palettes shown in Figure 2-3.

Next, let's take a look at your basic Painter 2016 user interface elements and see how these compare to Inkscape.

Painter: Tour of the Basic User Interface

Launch Painter using the quick launch icon on the taskbar that you created in Chapter 1. The user interface, as seen in Figure 2-4, has more than a dozen primary areas that you need to be concerned with, and another dozen specialized areas that we'll be getting into over the course of this book. These include menus, Brush Selections, Brush Options, Assets Toolbar, Painter Toolbar, Layers, Channels, Navigator, Color Wheel, Color Mixer, Color Set Libraries, Brush Flow Maps, Flow Map Libraries, and the Auto-Painting settings floating palette.

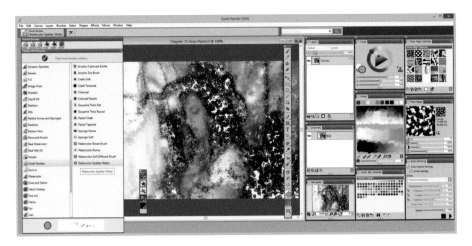

Figure 2-4. *Some of the primary Painter user interface elements*

We will be opening all of the other floating palettes in Painter over the course of this book, and learning what each of them do, so I am not going to try and cover this voluminous GUI in one chapter, as you need to master these features over time.

Summary

In this second chapter I made sure you had a solid foundational understanding of vector illustration and raster image concepts, since these both come together in digital painting software. We also took a bird's eye view of both Inkscape and Corel Painter user interfaces, so that you could see the different things you would be using and learning about over the course of this book.

In Chapter 3 you'll take a closer look at **brush stroke technologies** for both Inkscape 0.91 as well as for Corel Painter 2016, since I want to get to brushes (digital painting) as early on in the book as possible.

■ ■ ■

CHAPTER 3

The Foundation of Digital Painting: Canvas and Brush

Now that you have learned about the vector and raster concepts underlying digital painting software as well as taken a tour of the Inkscape and Painter 2016 user interfaces on your digital painting workstations, I want to cover the core topics of using **brushes** on your **canvas**, which is called a **page** in Inkscape. I'm going to cover this using both your open source (free) software package, as well as using your professional-level software, or your free trial version, so that we can continue to cover more and more advanced topics as this book progresses onwards. I'll cover topics in both Inkscape and Painter whenever possible; however some digital painting features have not yet been added to Inkscape, so some chapters will only feature Corel Painter.

We will look at how to implement Inkscape brush strokes, which is surprisingly robust at digital painting for an SVG XML generation software package, as well as in Corel Painter 2016.

Inkscape Brush Strokes: Digital Painting

Inkscape hasn't put an emphasis on brush-based digital painting in the way Corel Painter has, as you can tell in Figure 3-1, by noticing the **fountain pen** that is currently being used for the Inkscape **Draw Calligraphic or Brush Strokes** tool. That being said, there are almost a dozen different settings for the brush stroke design work process, as well as a Presets drop-down menu where you can store handy brushes or use brushes that Inkscape offers. Inkscape is making some strides in this area of digital painting. What is even more significant is the Inkscape support for digital painting tablets and stylus hardware, with settings for stylus pressure and stylus angle data. Anyone who tells you Inkscape does not support or focus on brush strokes and digital painting needs to take a look at the Inkscape 0.91 **Draw Brush Strokes Setting Bar**, which can be seen in Figure 3-1, and which we'll be looking at in detail in this section of the chapter.

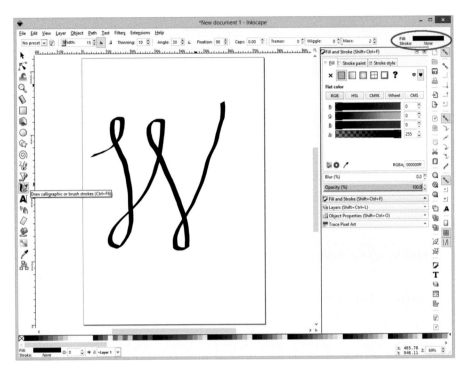

Figure 3-1. Using Inkscape's Draw calligraphic or brush strokes tool to draw a "W"

Calligraphy Brush Stroke Tool: Basic Style Setting

Open Inkscape and select the Draw calligraphic or brush strokes tool from the toolbar, and draw a brush stroke on your page. Inkscape is more digital illustration than digital paint oriented, so the canvas is called the page in Inkscape. As you can see in Figure 3-1, you click on **Fill** and **Stroke** indicators, at the far right of the **Brush Stroke Setting Bar,** at the top of Inkscape, to configure the style for your brush stroke, which I will configure to look like a **black magic marker** paint stroke.

Click the Fill and Stroke indicator color bar circled in red on the right-hand side of Figure 3-1. This will open up the **Preferences ➤ Calligraphy** dialog, which is shown in Figure 3-2.

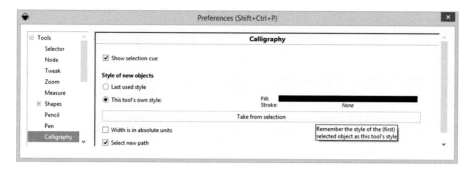

Figure 3-2. *Set Brush Stroke Calligraphy in Preferences dialog*

I checked the **Show selection cue** and the **Select new path** tool helper options, as you can see, and I set the **Style of new objects** option "This tool's own style." You will set these Fill and Stroke indicators on the right by using a button underneath them labeled "Take from selection," which copies a style from a selection. I set my brush tool to black so I can see it better.

You can set the style characteristics for a brush stroke after you draw it, by selecting the stroke with the **arrow** tool.

I drew a W using the Brush Strokes tool, shown in Figures 3-1 and 3-3, and then I selected it and left the **Fill** as **Black**, and I set the **Stroke style** to **2 pixels** and the **Stroke paint** to a **Magenta** value, by using an RGB color value of **Red 216** (85%), **Green 0**, and **Blue 216** (85%). I cut and pasted this Stroke style dialog over the Inkscape page (canvas) to show these settings.

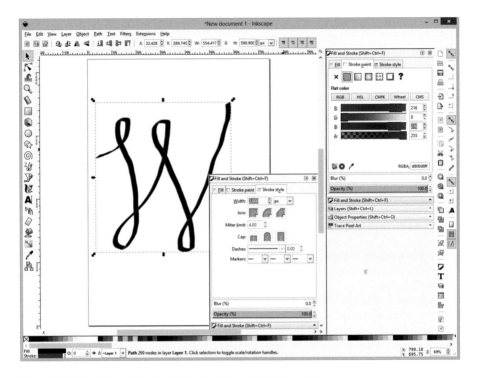

Figure 3-3. *Style brush stroke in Stroke style and Stroke paint*

Now that we have covered the basics of stroke colors and styling, let's take a look at the stroke dynamics settings that allow Inkscape to do at least a little of what Painter does for digital painting artists using a digital illustration workflow.

Brush Strokes Configuration: Advanced Settings

If you don't want to design custom Inkscape brush stroke dynamics configurations, which is what you'll be learning about in this section, you can use brush stroke presets, shown on the left side of Figure 3-4, in the brush drop-down menu selector.

Figure 3-4. *Brush Stroke preset, stylus pressure, and Stroke Cap*

Also shown, selected in blue, on the left side of Figure 3-4, is your "Use the pressure of the input device to alter the width of the pen" option toggle icon. This affords Inkscape the ability to use the digital painting tablet and stylus hardware.

Also shown selected in blue, and with the yellow tool tip pop-up helper message showing, is the **Caps** spinner. This allows you to make the caps at the end of your brush strokes protrude, more than they otherwise would. Use caps for a visual painting guide, to help you lay down the brush stroke you want to paint.

There's another feature toggle icon, seen on the left in Figure 3-5, which automates a tracing process by looking at the background contrast (light versus dark) and adjusting the brush width to match pixel contrast (darkness), making traces easier.

Figure 3-5. *The Trace lightness icon, Fixation, and Mass setting*

The **Mass** setting, shown on the right side of the screen, adds mass to your brush stroke, which makes the pen **drag behind** a stroke. The higher the value you set, the more drag you get.

As you know from physics, mass allows any object to have **inertia**. The higher you set the Mass spinner value for Inkscape calligraphic tool, the more it will smooth out sharp turns and quick jerks in the brush strokes. The default value (of 2) for the setting is initially set small so that the tool is fast and responsive, but you can increase this Mass spinner value, which results in a slow moving and thus smoother stylus brush stroke.

The **fixation** parameter seen highlighted in Figure 3-5 in blue in the middle of the screen controls your level of stroke contrast between thin and thick strokes, based on stylus angle.

A fixation value of **0** means that a brush angle is always constant, and so the stroke will be uniform, no matter what the stylus angle. This could be said to give the **least calligraphic** effect and so you'll get a very non-calligraphic stroke, as can be seen in Figure 3-1, where I used a very small setting of 16.

A fixation value of **100** means that a brush stroke should rotate freely, resulting in a stroke perpendicular to the stylus, like a fountain pen. This results in an exaggerated calligraphy stroke, as can be seen in Figure 3-6, where I used the fixation setting of 100, shown circled in red, at the top of the screen.

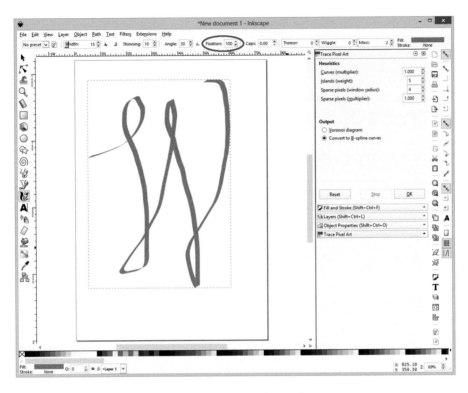

Figure 3-6. *Fixation setting of 100 gives a calligraphic stroke*

Decreasing a fixation value allows your calligraphic pen to turn less and less relative to the direction of your stroke.

The third feature toggle icon, which has what looks like a protractor on it, can be seen in blue in the middle of Figure 3-7. This turns on your tablet stylus hardware **tilt** feature. If you turn this on, your **Angle spinner** will be **dimmed**, as you can see, because the tilt of your stylus is controlling this value.

Figure 3-7. *Stylus tilt toggle icon and Wiggle slider setting*

Your **Wiggle** slider controls the **waver** and wiggle of your brush stroke, and is akin to the resistance of your page to the movement of your stylus (or mouse). The default is set to zero, the minimum value possible, and increasing this parameter makes your page surface (canvas) more and more slippery. If your Mass setting has a high data value, the stylus will tend to run away when sharp turns are implemented. If your Mass setting is zero, high Wiggle value will make the brush stroke waver erratically.

The last two settings, seen selected in blue, and with a tool tip pop-up deployed in Figure 3-8, are the **Thinning** spinner and the **Tremor** slider. The Tremor slider's there to control the slight wavering common with calligraphic strokes. Tremor ranges from 0 to 100, producing anything from slight unevenness (1–16) to many blotches and splotches (84–100). A proper use of Tremor will significantly expand your creative usage of a Brush tool.

Figure 3-8. *The Thinning spinner setting and the Tremor slider*

If you set the Thinning parameter to a nonzero value, a brush stroke's width can vary with velocity, controlled by this Thinning parameter. The parameter value ranges from -**100 to +100** with positive values making rapid strokes thinner, and negative values making rapid strokes broader. The default value is **0.10** and implements a very moderate thinning of fast brush strokes. You will need to experiment with these settings to master them!

Painter 2016 Brushes: Dynamic Painting

As amazing as it is that Inkscape has a brush stroke tool that uses pressure and tilt sensitive stylus and table hardware, and therefore will allow digital painting to be performed with open source software, there's a paid software package that is taking digital painting to all new levels year after year. The latest Painter revision was released just in time for me to be able to include coverage of this vanguard new digital painting software and its advanced algorithmic features for this new media title.

Types of Digital Painting: Painter 2016 Workflows

Painter has several ways of approaching the creation of your digital painting, which is termed "workflows." In essence these are much of what this entire book will be about, so we will only cover one of these workflows in the hands-on example in the chapter. The most complex of the Painter workflows involves starting with a blank canvas and using all the brushes to paint your artwork from scratch. The least complex is a workflow that starts with a **File ➤ Quick Clone** menu sequence and uses one brush with the **Auto-Painting** feature, which we will do later on in this chapter, just to get you up and running quickly in only the third chapter of this book. The other workflows fall somewhere in between the two digital painting asset generation extremes (100% manual painting versus 100% automated painting).

One of the most popular workflows in Painter is using an image as a guide for brush colors. Color is taken from a source image and then painted by the user onto a **cloned image canvas**, using the **File ➤ Clone** menu sequence. I will show you this work process, in its own chapter in the book. Another workflow is to use a sketch, possibly a digital illustration with no stroke or fills implemented, as a guide to paint on. You can also utilize Painter's tracing features to create this interim sketch, using a photograph, and then use that as your digital painting guide.

Automatic Painting: Using Painter's Auto-Painting

I'm going to show you how to have Painter do all of the digital painting work, using the **Auto-Painting** floating palette, in conjunction with the **Underpainting** floating palette. The first thing that you will need to do, as you can see in Figure 3-9, is open an image that you want to create a digital painting out of using the **File ➤ Open** menu sequence. Find the **Niki.png** image in the book repository and open it. This Niki image is a PNG24 from my *Digital Image Compositing* (Apress, 2015) title, which I wrote earlier this year. Next, use your **File ➤ Quick Clone** menu sequence, as shown in Figure 3-9, and set up your cloned image.

Figure 3-9. *Invoke the Painter File ➤ Quick Clone menu sequence*

This menu sequence will create and open your quick clone window, which I then saved, by using a **Chapter-3-Auto-Paint.rif** filename. This menu sequence will also open up the **Clone Source** floating palette, with **Niki** in it, as is shown in Figure 3-10.

Figure 3-10. *Clone Source floating palette appears showing Niki*

Next, drop down your **Painter Brushes** selector and select the **Smart Strokes** Group, selecting the **Watercolor Spatter Water** brush, from the right side of this drop-down menu, as shown in Figure 3-11. There's a preview of what the brush will look like located at the bottom of the Painter Brushes drop-down selector user interface, so you can preview the effect of these brushes.

Figure 3-11. *Select Smart Strokes ➤ Watercolor Spatter Water*

33

To get Painter to create your digital painting asset for you automatically, click on the **Play** button I circled in Figure 3-11, until you get the result that you like. After that, click on the **Stop** button, shown highlighted in blue, with the tool tip pop-up showing underneath it, in Figure 3-12.

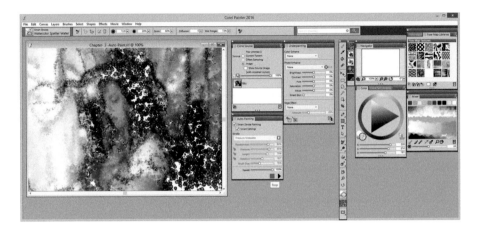

Figure 3-12. *Click Play and Stop icons to control Auto-Paint*

As you are starting to realize after only three chapters in this book, Painter 2016 is an extremely advanced algorithmic digital painting engine, one which content producers would need to put in years of practice, to master its impressive features.

If you want to create original artwork for your clients, mastering Painter should be well worth your time, and a lot of fun to explore during that process anyway! I suggest mastering this powerful paint and illustration software, and then adding it to your multimedia content production tool set.

Although we are covering almost as much about Inkscape digital painting features during this book as well, since the Inkscape software is open source, the majority of the content within the book will relate to the more advanced digital painting features that are found in Corel Painter 2016.

If you wanted to explore digital illustration features, and Inkscape more than Painter, then the book that does this is the *Digital Illustration Fundamentals* (Apress, 2015) title. This title covers SVG commands and the vector components of Inkscape much more than the raster components of digital painting, which this book covers in greater detail.

These two books together cover the entire spectrum of an illustration to painting crossover that has happened in popular software packages such as CorelDRAW and Corel Painter 2016, and I assume in Inkscape as time goes on, as that software package adds more and more digital painting features that bridge vector illustration to raster imaging, using digital painting engines and digital painting algorithms.

Summary

In this third chapter, we covered using a canvas, or page in Inkscape, as well as brushes and brush strokes in both Inkscape as well as in Corel Painter 2016. First we went over the basics of vector illustration concepts such as vertices, lines, and curves, and then we reviewed raster imaging concepts such as pixels, resolution, aspect ratio, color channels, color depth, alpha channel, anti-aliasing, blending modes, and the like, which are used to some extent in Inkscape and even more so in Painter. Next we looked at the Inkscape **Draw calligraphic and brush strokes** tool and its settings in the first half of the chapter. After that, we looked at the primary Painter workflows and then learned about the automatic digital painting workflow using Painter 2016's **Quick Clone** with **Auto-Painting**. This is an automated digital painting engine workflow in Painter and the logical workflow to cover first, to give readers a taste of digital painting within the first few chapters of the book. In Chapter 4 we will look at fill, stroke, and pattern vector concepts as well as using seamless digital imagery tiles in Inkscape as well as in Corel Painter 2016.

■■■

CHAPTER 4

Digital Painting with Image Tiles: Patterns and Weaves

Now that we have covered the basic concepts regarding vector and raster imagery as well as using brush strokes on a canvas (or page, in Inkscape), let's take a look at how to use patterns (Inkscape and Painter) and weaves (Painter) to fill areas with seamless image "tiles." We will review how to **stroke** and **fill** vector (closed path) objects, using both solid colors as well as **gradients**. The bulk of this chapter will cover the more complex 2D image seamless tile texturing **patterns** available in Inkscape as well as **weaves**, available in Painter.

I'll include a work process for the creation of seamless tiling image patterns. These are more effective, or believable, than patterns where you see a repeating seam. Certain patterns, such as plaid or polka dots, are inherently tilable, by their very nature. In the chapter we'll look at how to create **bitmap image tiles** using GIMP 2.8, which can be used with Inkscape or Painter as patterns, weaves or nozzles, and how to apply them to vector illustration in Inkscape or to raster brush strokes in Painter.

Inkscape Styles: Stroke, Fill, and Gradient

Let's make sure you have the basics regarding how to style your Inkscape object using stroke, fill, and gradient before we get into patterns. Painter has gradients as well, so all of what we will do here with Inkscape also applies to Painter as well. Launch Inkscape with **Digital_Painting_Techniques_CH4_Stroke.svg** or use the **File ➤ Open** menu sequence, and click on the **Arrow** selection tool and select the Heart object and the Stroke style tab, where you can set the Width of the stroke, shown selected in Figure 4-1. I created this custom SVG object in the *Digital Illustration Fundamentals* (Apress, 2015) title. A stroke command will add thickness to the lines or curves that make up your 2D vector objects. This is true in either Inkscape or in Painter. I set the Stroke Width to 5 pixels, to create this empty heart.

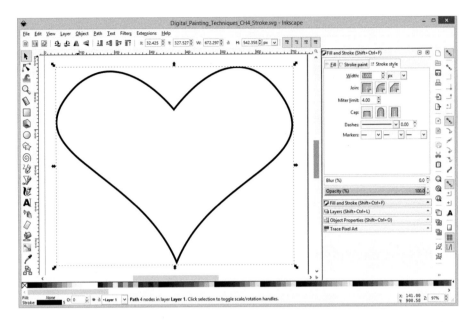

Figure 4-1. Open CH4_Stroke.svg and select the Stroke style tab and set Width to 5 pixels

Click the **Fill** tab, seen selected in Figure 4-2, and the **solid color icon**, and select **RGB** color and set a **Red 192** value.

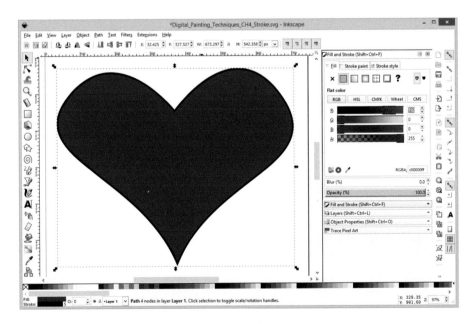

Figure 4-2. Select Fill tab, click Solid icon, set Red to 192

If you select a **Radial Gradient Fill Icon**, seen selected on the right side of Figure 4-3, you will get a gradient in the center of the heart vector object, which also looks quite nice.

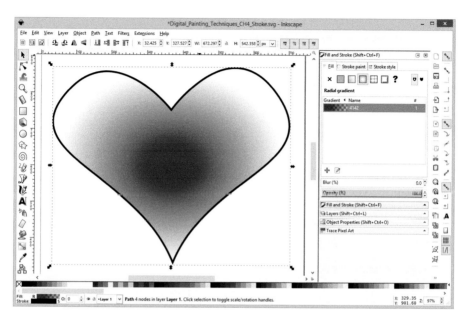

Figure 4-3. *Click a Radial Gradient Icon and Red to Transparent*

Before we look at **Pattern Fills**, the first thing that we will need to learn is how to use GIMP 2.8.14 to create a bitmap pattern that we can use in either Inkscape or in Corel Painter.

Using GIMP: Creating Your Image Pattern

If you have not downloaded and installed the open source GIMP 2.8.14 digital image editing and compositing software yet, go to http://www.gimp.org, and click the orange **Download** button, and then install the software on your digital painting workstation. After you've installed GIMP, launch it, and let's get to work!

Click your **background color swatch**, shown circled on the right side of Figure 4-4. You can tell by an icon that white is your background color currently, because it appears as if it is **behind** the black (foreground) color icon. This is numbered with a one in Figure 4-4, and shows a **Change Background Color** picker dialog below it. I set a color Hue value of **zero**, **48%** saturation, and **96%** lightness value, which equates to RGB values of **Red 245** (96% Red), **Green 127** (50% Green), and **Blue 127** (50% Blue). These values will give you a nice "Teaberry" heart background color.

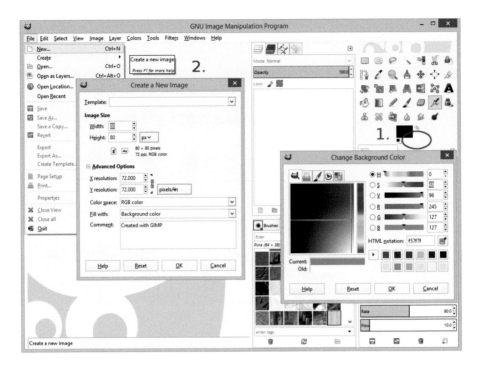

Figure 4-4. *Open GIMP; set background color; create a new image*

Step two, seen on the left side of Figure 4-4, is to use a **File ➤ New** menu sequence and open the GIMP **Create a New Image** dialog. Set an **80 pixel** Width and Height using a **72 DPI** X and Y resolution, and specify the **RGB Color Space**.

Set **Fill with** to **Background color**. This is why you set up your Teaberry background color as step one in the work process.

As you can see in Figure 4-5, your Background layer now has an appropriate background color for your heart object, and you can select a circular area using a circle and ellipse tool. This tool is shown selected in blue at the top right of Figure 4-5 in the **tool icons palette** of GIMP. In the **Tool Options** tab under the tool icons, I selected **Antialiasing**, and **Expand from center** as tool options, and drew out a circular selection area. I also clicked the **foreground color swatch** and set that to **Red**.

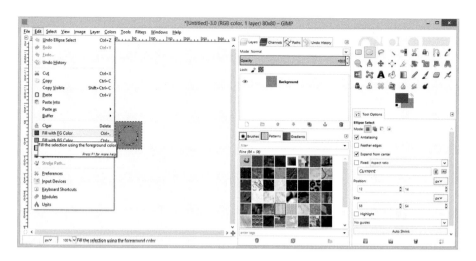

Figure 4-5. *Select circular area; use Edit ➤ Fill with FG Color*

The circular selection area is shown on the left side of your screen, as is the **Edit ➤ Fill with FG Color** menu sequence, which is what you should use to tell GIMP to fill the selection you just created with a Red color for your Heart object pattern fill, which you are creating here using digital image software.

If you want the Red circle on a **different layer** than the background color, just to provide you with a little taste of my GIMP 2.8.14 knowledge, outlined in my *Digital Image Compositing Fundamentals* (Apress, 2015) title I wrote previous to this one, click on the **Background** layer to select it and then right-click and select a **New Layer** context-sensitive menu option. This will instruct GIMP to create a new layer to hold your Red Circle.

Be sure that you create this new layer **before** you invoke your **Edit ➤ Fill** menu sequence, so that you are directing GIMP to place your Red Fill Color on the new layer instead of over the background fill color on the **Background** fill layer.

Whichever work process (one layer or two layers) you use is fine to achieve this same result, so pick one, implement it, and then utilize the **Select ➤ None** menu sequence to remove this selection, now that you have used it to create your Red Circle. This menu sequence can be seen in Figure 4-6, on the left side, along with the tool tip pop-up helper (seen in pale yellow) that will tell you what each of the GIMP menu items, tool icons, and user interface elements will do for a digital image editing and compositing workflow.

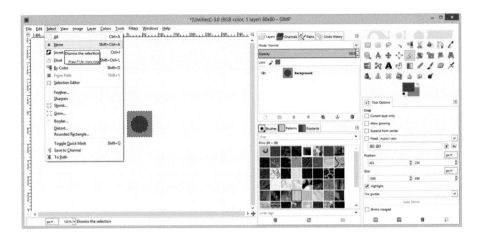

Figure 4-6. *Deselect circle, using Select ➤ None menu sequence*

This is a great way to quickly learn what these features in GIMP, or any other new media software, for that matter, will do for your multimedia content production work process.

I'll try to cover the major visual (2D) new media genres in this book, as they are all interrelated. Inkscape is digital illustration, GIMP is digital image compositing, and Painter is digital painting, although each of these shares common aspects.

As you can see in the **Layers** tab in the middle I decided to use my Background layer to hold my pattern composition. Next use the **File ➤ Export As** menu sequence, shown in Figure 4-7, to export (save) this pattern in the PNG bitmap image file format.

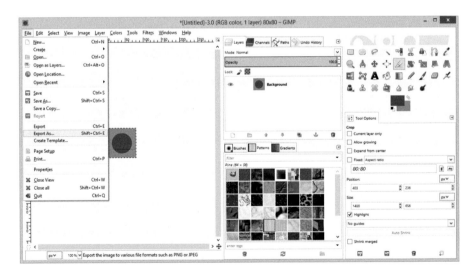

Figure 4-7. *Use File ➤ Export As to save a pattern as a bitmap*

In the Export Image dialog, type the **PolkaHeart.png** file name in the Name field at the top of the dialog.

Your extension for your filename, that is, the **.PNG** part of the filename, will inform GIMP 2.8 which bitmap file format, or encoding algorithm, that you want your image data to use. I prefer the lossless .PNG (pronounced "Ping") image data format, as it provides the best visual results with great compression.

Click on the **Export** button to export your bitmap pattern to the directory on your hard disk drive that you selected with the **Places** pane of the Export Image dialog on the far left. The folder hierarchy I used was E:\Digital_Painting_Techniques\CH04.

The next thing that we need to do is to show you how you can install these custom bitmap image patterns inside Inkscape.

Using Imagery in Painting and Illustration

Now that I've shown you how to utilize the popular open source GIMP digital image compositing software to create a tilable bitmap image pattern for use inside of Inkscape or Painter 2016 it's time to show you the work process for installing your own custom bitmap image artwork, so that you can **bridge** your work in digital image compositing software with digital illustration and digital painting software genres. This will allow you to **leverage** your digital image compositing pipeline with your digital illustration content creation pipeline and your digital painting artwork creation pipeline. Inkscape will fuse bitmaps and vectors together using its SVG command generation engine, which I cover in *Digital Illustration Fundamentals* (Apress, 2015). More advanced 2D illustration software that supports advanced digital painting workflows, such as Corel Painter 2016 will bridge bitmap (raster) with vector using even more advanced features.

Using Bitmap Images as Fill: Inkscape Pattern Fill

Let's use a bitmap-based fill pattern this time to add far more visual interest to a vector heart object than I created using Bézier Splines in the *Digital Illustration Fundamentals* book. Open Inkscape using the Digital_Painting_Techniques_CH4.svg project from this book's repository. You can do this by double-clicking on the file in your file manager, or right-click the file and use **Open with Inkscape**, or use **File ➤ Open** in Inkscape. Use the **File ➤ Import** menu sequence, as seen in Figure 4-8, to open the **Select file to import** dialog. Navigate to, and then select, the **PolkaHeart.png** file, and then click the **Open** button, which will then open the **png bitmap image import** dialog seen at the bottom right side of Figure 4-8.

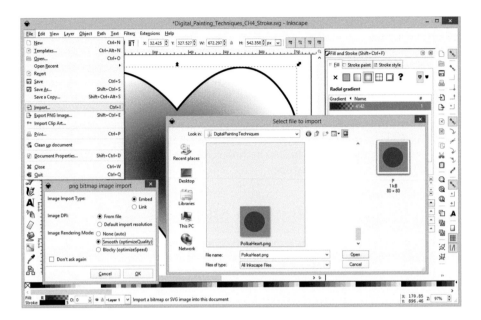

Figure 4-8. *Use File ➤ Import; select Embed and Smooth options*

Select the **Embed Image Import Type**, and select the **Image DPI From file** radio button option as well. I suggest using your **Smooth (optimizeQuality)** setting for your **Image Rendering Mode**, and I leave **don't ask again** unchecked, so I will always specify my preference for the SVG command language syntax that Inkscape is going to generate.

Once all of these settings have been specified, click on the **OK** button and you should see your bitmap pattern tile asset in the middle of Inkscape; in this case, it will probably be on top of the Heart object. Select the image tile using the arrow, or selection, tool, then drag it out of the way of your digital illustration, as is shown in the lower right-hand corner of the page (canvas) in Figure 4-9.

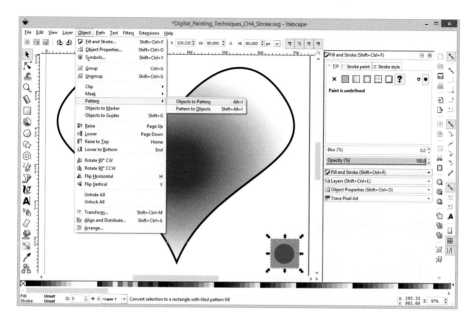

Figure 4-9. *Use Object ➤ Pattern ➤ Objects to Pattern menu sequence*

The next step in the work process, also shown at the top of Figure 4-9, is to use Inkscape's **Object ➤ Pattern ➤ Objects to Pattern** menu sequence, to invoke the Inkscape function that converts bitmap objects into patterns that can be used in fill and stroke operations.

Make sure that your image tile is selected before you do this step, as your selection would show this Objects to Pattern algorithm what to install in the Patterns (drop-down) selector. Then you can click your heart object and select it for editing.

In the Inkscape **Stroke and Fill** palette, select the **Fill** tab, and then select the **Pattern icon**, as shown in Figure 4-10.

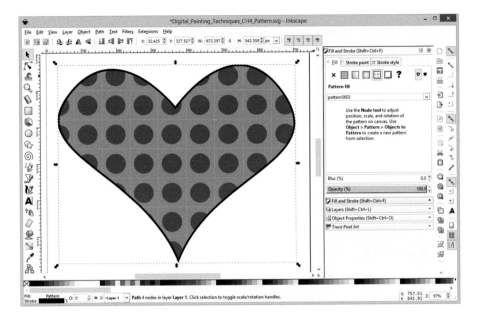

Figure 4-10. *A bitmap image pattern will fill the heart shape*

In the Pattern fill section of the dialog, use the drop-down menu to select your pattern5603 option, which is what the SVG command syntax generator named the pattern in the previous Objects to Pattern function. This may be a different number in your version of Inkscape; in fact it probably will be different as it is generated based on some internal Inkscape algorithm.

The pattern should appear in your top-most recently used patterns portion of the drop-down selector because you recently added it to the Inkscape project. As you can see in Figure 4-10, the heart now looks great!

Next, let's take a quick look at how patterns and weaves are used in Corel Painter, to bridge raster and vector as well.

Bitmaps in Painting: Painter Patterns and Weaves

Corel Painter 2016 also supports patterns, as well as gradients and something called "weaves." We will go over these in this section of the chapter so you can see that Painter supports the vector illustration content pipeline (workflow) as well as your raster-based digital image compositing and digital painting workflows. As you might have guessed, patterns can not only be filled in Painter, but they can also be painted on your canvas, which we'll be covering in more advanced chapters on painting.

I have used the **File ➤ Export PNG Image** menu sequence in Inkscape to open the **Export PNG Image** palette, shown in Figure 4-11. I used a default filename and clicked the **Export** button.

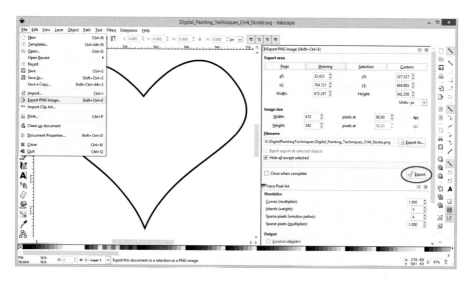

Figure 4-11. *Use Export PNG Image to export heart object as PNG*

In this way, the PNG file has the same name as your .SVG file that Inkscape uses for your heart project. I also accepted the default Width of 672 pixels and Height of 542 pixels. These vector projects in Inkscape can be "rendered" at any resolution you like, with the same high-quality level across the board.

Now let's launch Painter 2016 and use a **File ➤ Open** menu sequence to open your Digital_Painting_Techniques_CH4_Stroke.png file.

Your heart object, with your 5-pixel stroke, transparent background, and its own **Layer 1** layer, is now highlighted as an active layer, in green, on top of a **Canvas** layer in the Painter **Layers** palette, as you can see on the left and middle in Figure 4-12. Also seen on the bottom left in Figure 4-12 is a floating toolbar containing patterns, gradients, and weaves. I've clicked on the patterns icon drop-down arrow to open a **Painter Patterns** selector and found an appropriate pink **Lotus Petals** pattern to use to fill the center of the heart object created in Inkscape.

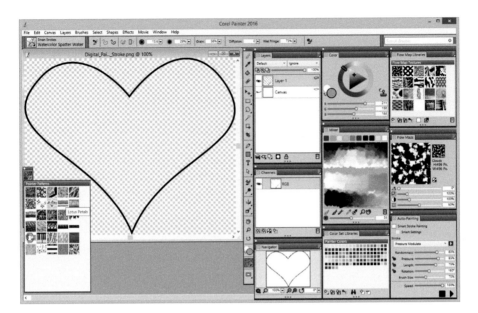

Figure 4-12. *Use File ➤ Open to open a heart object in Painter and select Lotus Petals pattern*

Next, with the Layer 1 layer selected, click on the tool that has a pouring paint can on it (the Fill tool) and click in the center of the heart object. This will fill the heart with a Lotus Petals pattern, as is seen on the top-left side in Figure 4-13. I have circled the **Fill Tool Icon** in red in the figure as well, and you can see that your **Navigator** floating palette and your Layers palette **Layer 1** icon now reflect your new artwork. The result is visually stimulating using professional graphics.

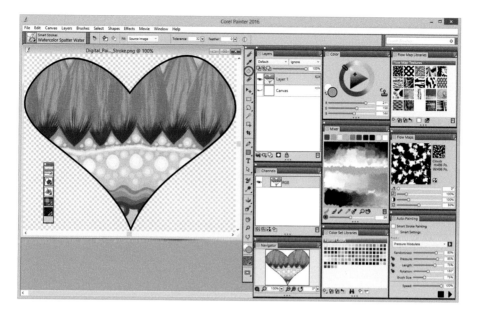

Figure 4-13. *Select Fill (Paint Can) tool; click inside heart*

Next, we will take a closer look at Painter 2016 weaves, which are also accessed via the Painter Assets floating toolbar seen in Figure 4-13 on the lower left. The patterns use the top icon, whereas Painter weaves use the fourth icon from the top.

Use an **Edit ➤ Undo Paint Bucket Fill** menu sequence that will undo this pattern fill operation that you just performed, and select the Weaves icon, in the Painter Assets toolbar. This will drop down the Painter Weaves selector, which can be seen in Figure 4-14, on the bottom left-hand side.

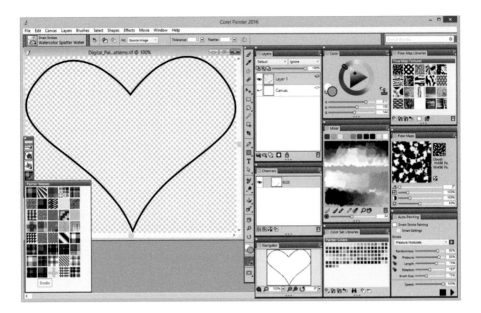

Figure 4-14. *Use Edit* ➤ *Undo Paint Bucket Fill to clear heart, and select Brodie Weave*

I selected the heart appropriate "Brodie" weave, as seen in the pop-up tool tip underneath this weave sample icon, as you can see at the bottom of Figure 4-14 on the left-hand side.

Then I made sure that Layer 1 layer was selected and I clicked on the Fill tool, and then I clicked in the center of the heart object. This filled the heart with a Brodie weave, as is seen on the top-left side in Figure 4-15. I have circled the Fill Tool Icon in red in Figure 4-13 in case you already forgot where it was located in the Corel Painter 2016 user interface.

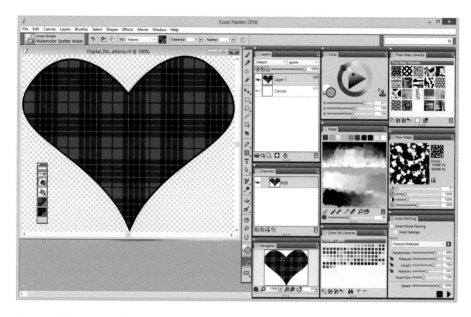

Figure 4-15. *Select Fill (Paint Can) tool; click inside heart*

You can again see that your Navigator floating palette, as well as your Layers palette Layer 1 icon, now reflects your new plaid heart artwork. Pretty cool graphics, if you ask me!

Your Brodie weave paint fill can be seen in Figure 4-15.

Finally, just to be thorough, let's try using this exact same work process using the Painter Rainbow Pinch gradient from the Painter Gradients section of the Painter Assets toolbar. As is shown in Figure 4-16, a gradient will emanate from where you click your paint bucket fill tool inside of your heart object.

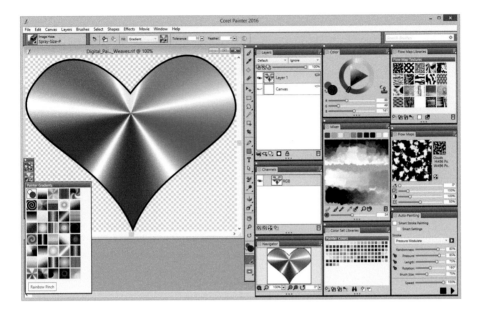

Figure 4-16. *Fill a heart object using a Rainbow Pinch gradient*

Now we've covered gradients, patterns, and weaves in both Inkscape and Painter, so we have covered the rest of the vector concepts of strokes, fills, patterns, and gradients.

Summary

In this fourth chapter, we looked at how you can use patterns and weaves to add digital imagery to the fills for your 2D vector illustration shapes in Inkscape and Painter. Inkscape can also perform strokes using these patterns as well, as covered in my *Digital Illustration Fundamentals* (Apress, 2015) title. We looked at the work process for using the GIMP digital image compositing software package to create tiles to use as bitmap patterns, as well as at the work process for importing and applying them inside of Inkscape; and using patterns, gradients, and weaves in Corel Painter.

In the next chapter, you will take a look at **tablets** and **stylus hardware** and how these can be installed and utilized.

■ ■ ■

CHAPTER 5

The Hardware of Digital Painting: Tablet and Stylus

Now that we have covered the basic concepts regarding vector illustration and how you can bridge it over to raster imagery, before we get heavily into brush dynamics and all of that complex digital painting fare, let's take a look at the hardware products that could facilitate your digital painting workflow. During this chapter, we'll take a look at some of the different types of **pressure-sensitive stylus** products, as well as the more advanced and professional **tablet with stylus** solutions. We will look at some of the platforms that support the digital painting hardware products, as well as how to install and use one of the leading hardware manufacturer's digital painting products.

Digital Painting Hardware: Pen and Tablet

Let's start with the stylus hardware component, sometimes called a "digital pen" for your digital painting workflow; without this hardware, you will not be able to generate any pressure-sensitive digital painting data. This is because current mouse hardware does not generate pressure data and neither will your fingertip, or even a solid plastic or metal stylus that comes with some **Phablets** such as my Samsung Galaxy Note. A Phablet is a Phone-Tablet hybrid device. Due to the proliferation of tablets and eBook readers such as the iPad and Kindle Fire, pressure-sensitive stylus products that will work with touchscreen displays have recently become available for iOS, Android or Windows smartphones, tablets, eBook Readers, and powerful touchscreen laptop computers, such as the recent Microsoft Surface and Surface Pro products that run Windows 10.

Although there are a lot of manufacturers out there that make these products, I am going to cover your most professional solutions, the ones I use from international company **Wacom (**www.wacom.com**)**. We will start with pressure-sensitive stylus products, compatible with touchscreen devices, and then get into specialized tablets.

Pressure-Sensitive Stylus: Digital Pens for Mobile

There's a genre of digital painting hardware that works across popular touchscreen consumer electronics devices running iOS or Android, called a pressure-sensitive stylus or digital pen. The pressure-sensitive stylus supports pressure data and can be far less expensive than full-blown digital painting hardware, which we will cover in the next section of the chapter. Because there is only the stylus component of the product and no tablet part needed to receive the X,Y point location data, a touchscreen serves as the tablet part of the stylus-tablet product combination. Most Phones or Tablets have advanced touchscreen support, which has made the stylus product possible, and due to the billions of touchscreen devices in the marketplace, the pressure-sensitive stylus is steadily growing in both popularity and product sales.

Figure 5-1 shows a recent Wacom Intuos Creative Stylus 2 product in use with the Apple iPad tablet, which as you can see in Figure 5-1, allows you to paint directly on your artwork.

Figure 5-1. *Wacom Intuos Creative Stylus 2 in use with an iPad*

Figure 5-2 shows an even clearer angle of a stylus being used on the surface of a touchscreen tablet. The rubber tip for the stylus will record and transmit pressure data, and position data (X,Y location) is handled by the touchscreen itself, as it usually does using a solid (non-electronic) stylus or fingertip in normal everyday usage.

A thinner, firmer tip draws more naturally and lasts much longer.

Intuos Creative Stylus 2   Intuos Creative Stylus

Figure 5 2. *Wacom is continually improving their stylus product*

Wacom is continually improving both the durability and the quality of its stylus and tablet products, as you can see, on the right-hand side of Figure 5-2. Wacom's **Intuos Stylus 2** product clearly is better designed, looks more streamlined, and easier to hold, uses a superior protected tip, and now supports higher-resolution screens, for finer-stroked digital paintings.

If you're using a professional-level workstation such as the 64-bit AMD-8350 OctaCore that I am using, you are probably using True HD 1920x1080 or Ultra HD 3840x2160 (Quad HD) display screen hardware, which is usually not touchscreen. In this case you'll need to be using a more expensive tablet plus stylus setup, which is what we are going to be taking a look at next.

The Tablet with Pressure and Tilt Sensitive Stylus

The advantage of a tablet plus stylus pairing is that the two components work together as one unit. This allows not only X,Y location and pressure data, but also tilt and orientation data. As you can see in Figure 5-3, Wacom has a sleek and affordable Intuos Pro product line that spans a range of surface sizes.

Figure 5-3. *Wacom Intuos Pro series of digital painting tablets*

As you can see in Figure 5-4, the Wacom web site has some very detailed specifications on the Intuos Pro, including size, weight, colors, features, connection types (USB, and Wireless), and compatibility with either the Mac OSX and Windows OS, which is what I'm using my Wacom Intuos 4 on (Windows 8.1) currently.

Figure 5-4. *The Wacom Intuos Pro Medium product specifications*

As you can see in Figure 5-5, there is a wide variety of extras that you can get for the Intuos Pro, including different stylus components (called **Pens**, on Wacom's web site), as well as different **Nibs** (Replaceable Tips) and **Pen Grips** for your digital painting comfort, as well as **Kits** that contain "collections" of all of the different variants on these Nibs and Pen Grip items.

Figure 5-5. Wacom Intuos Pro offers a wide range of accessories

Next, let's take a look at your highest level of digital painting hardware, which can get into the thousands of dollars!

Touchscreen Tablet with Pressure and Tilt Stylus

The most expensive and highest-level digital painting hardware can combine all of these features in one product. These feature a high-resolution touchscreen display, as an integrated part of the product, as well as the pressure and tilt sensitive stylus. This will allow you to draw right on top of the artwork with extreme precision and artistic control. The Wacon products that provide this highest level of functionality are the Cintiq products, which can be seen in Figure 5-6 on the Wacom web site.

Figure 5-6. Wacom Cintiq Touchscreen Tablet with Stylus product

There are a range of Wacom Cintiq products that have the display integrated and which require your external computer to run the digital painting software, and there are several Cintiq products that have the computer right inside of them, allowing you to take a digital painting studio with you wherever you go!

The next thing that we need to do is to show you how you can install these digital painting hardware drivers in your OS.

Installing Digital Painting Hardware Driver

Now that I have shown you how wide ranging the digital painting hardware offerings are these days, I will show you how to find the correct device driver for your digital painting hardware and how to install it on your digital painting workstation. It is important to always have the latest drivers on your system, so perform the following work process at least once every six months or whenever there is an update to your tablet's drivers.

Find the Correct Driver: Google Search for Product

The first step is to open your browser – I used Google Chrome – and go to `www.google.com` and enter the search term that is comprised of three keywords: a **manufacturer name**, your **product name**, and the word "Driver." In my case, that equates to a search for "Wacom Intuos Driver" seen at the top of Figure 5-7.

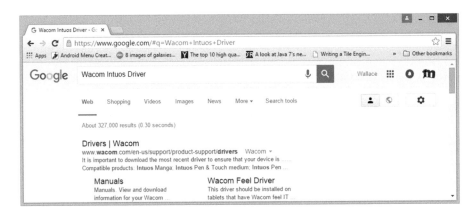

Figure 5-7. *Google Search for "[Manufacturer] [Product] Driver"*

Go to your manufacturer's site, select the **Drivers** page; select **Product Name** and **Type**, as seen at the top of Figure 5-8; and navigate over to the driver download page for your tablet.

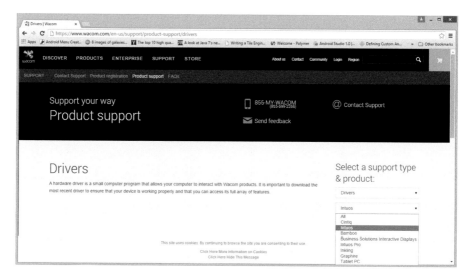

Figure 5-8. *Select the Drivers and Product Name/Type Categories*

Finally, click a download link or button for your tablet product, as is shown on the right-hand side in Figure 5-9.

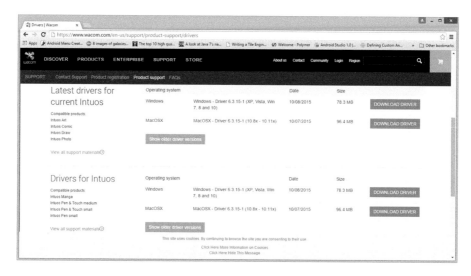

Figure 5-9. *Download the drivers for your tablet product model*

Once you've downloaded the driver installation files, you will be ready to install the tablet driver. Let's do that next.

Installing the Latest Driver: Run as Administrator

Locate and then right-click on the downloaded file, and select the **Run as Administrator** menu option, as shown in Figure 5-10.

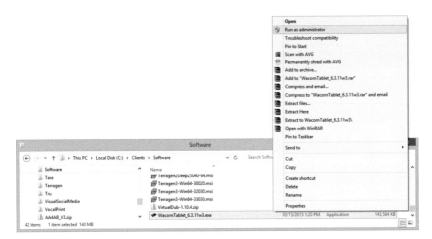

Figure 5-10. *Right-click the EXE and Run as Administrator*

Once you launch an installer it will extract the install files to your computer, as you can see on the left-hand side of Figure 5-11. You will then get a **License Agreement** dialog, seen on the right-hand side of Figure 5-11, where you can **Accept** the terms of the software licensing agreement.

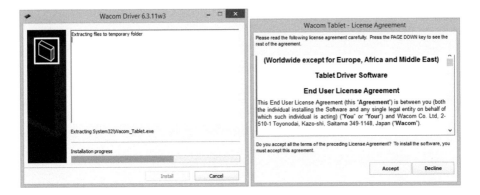

Figure 5-11. *Start the Install and Accept the License Agreement*

Once you accept the License Agreement, your installation process will continue, as seen on the left side in Figure 5-12.

Figure 5-12. *Wait for the installation to complete and restart*

Once the installation process has completed, you'll want to restart your computer. The reason for this is because these hardware drivers are installed at the time the operating system is started, so the only way to get these newer (latest) drivers loaded into your system memory is to restart your workstation.

Summary

In this fifth chapter, we looked at digital painting hardware, including how to install drivers for digital painting hardware.

In the next chapter, we will take a look at **Nozzles and how to use the Image Hose brush in Corel Painter 2016**.

CHAPTER 6

■ ■ ■

Digital Painting with Image Objects: Using Nozzles

Now that we have covered the stylus and tablet hardware that is used by digital painting professionals – but before we get heavy into brush dynamics and all of Painter's complex digital painting algorithms, physics, and fluid dynamics – let's take a look at one of the things that Painter added back when it was Fractal Design Painter: **Nozzles**. Since I've been a beta-tester and user of Painter since Version 1, I'm going to cover Painter features in the order that they were added to the software so that this book progresses in not only a logical, but in a timely fashion.

During this chapter, we'll take a look at how to use the Nozzles that come in Painter, how to get free Nozzles from the Web, and how to use a **Layers** palette to create digital painting compositions that keep certain design components separated from each other. I'll include the work process for the creation of a Nozzle you can use in Painter as well, so that you know how the Painter software can be used to create an **Image Hose** Nozzle.

Painter Nozzles: Painting with Imagery

One of the icons in the Painter assets toolbar that we did not cover in the previous chapter was the third one down, which has Painter Nozzles in it. Nozzles are used by Corel Painter 2016's Image Hose brush setting in the Painter Brushes drop-down menu. The Image Hose is a type of brush that lets you spray imagery onto your canvas. To learn how to use Nozzles, let's open your **Niki.png** image and paint some decorative elements over the nonsubject matter areas using the Image Hose brush in conjunction with some of the Nozzles that come preinstalled in Painter. I decided to use **PassionFlower Leaves** to provide a nice green base at the bottom of the image. To select this Nozzle, I used the Nozzles icon and clicked the triangle to open it, as shown in the middle of Figure 6-1. Next I clicked the Painter Brushes drop-down menu and selected the **Image Hose** brush and setting.

Figure 6-1. *Painter Nozzles are in the third Asset Toolbar Icon*

I selected the **Spray-Size-P** brush type, which varies the size based on Pressure (P). I created a **New Layer** using an icon at the bottom of the **Layers** palette and named it **Passion Flower Leaves**, as is shown circled in red in the middle of Figure 6-2.

Figure 6-2. *Select an Image Hose Brush, then Create a New Layer named PassionFlowerLeaves*

I set the brush size to **27.5** pixels, seen set at the top left in Figure 6-3. I then painted in some leaves at the bottom of the image. I then created a **Passion Flower Flowers** layer by using the Painter New Layer icon (again), as can be seen in the middle of Figure 6-3 in the Layers palette. I then dropped down the Painter Nozzles selector again using the Painter Asset icon shown in Figure 6-3 and selected the PassionFlower Flowers. You can see the pop-up tool tip in the middle of Figure 6-3.

Figure 6-3. *Paint Leaves, Select PassionFlowers, Create PassionFlowerFlowers Layer*

As you can see, on the right side of Figure 6-4, I then painted in some PassionFlower, and then created another layer that I named **Colorful Petals**, to hold the colored petals that I am going to fill in the upper-left corner of the Niki image.

Figure 6-4. *Paint PassionFlower Flowers and Colored Petals on separate layers*

I am doing this to finish off filling over some of these background imagery distractions for the digital portrait that I have decided to paint over with the Image Hose Nozzles, to show you how this innovative painting feature works.

Note in Figures 6-3 and 6-4 that I am placing each Nozzle type that I'm using on a **different layer**, so that I have the ability to preview, move, and apply special effects to each one individually. This is termed **multi-layer compositing**.

Before I add each different design element to my digital painting, I either invoke the **Layers ➤ New Layer** menu sequence, or click a **New Layer icon** at the bottom of your Layers palette, seen circled in red, in Figure 6-2. We will use multiple layers in the next section of the chapter to create Nozzles as well.

Next, let's get more advanced and take a look at how you can create your own Image Hose Nozzle, because I know you think that this particular aspect of Painter is really quite useful!

Creating Nozzles: Using Multiple Layers

Image Hose Nozzles that are created inside of Painter 2016 as Nozzles are inherently RIFF files. This is your "native" format for Corel Painter digital painting composition data structures. As you can see in Figure 6-5, the first step after you launch a Painter 2016 session is to use the **File ➤ New** menu sequence and use the **New Image** dialog to set your canvas resolution for your Nozzle, which you are about to create. I suggest you match your resolution to your target composition resolution usage; thus if you are going to paint a **1280x720** (BluRay) resolution image, use a 240x240 pixel canvas; for a **1920x1080 True HD** (iTV Set) image use a 480x480 pixel canvas, as I am here; and for **UHD 4096x2160** imagery, or print resolution imagery, use the 960x960 canvas or even higher resolution if you're working on highway billboards.

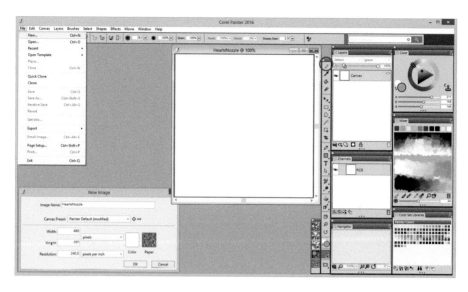

Figure 6-5. *Create 480 pixel resolution canvas, 240 PPI density*

Name your new image **HeartNozzle**, as shown in Figure 6-5, and then select a **Brush Tool** at the top of the Painter toolbar. This tool is the one which you can use to create **Bézier curves**, like the Draw Bézier tool in Inkscape, and so let's take a look at how to create spline-based vector shape objects in Painter.

Creating Vector Shapes in Painter: The Brush Tool

Interestingly, not only is the Painter Brush Tool used for your digital painting strokes, but it can also be used to create the vector shape artwork for your digital painting compositions. As I was mentioning earlier in the book, digital painting engines build raster styling and effects on top of vector illustration foundational artwork, which you're about to see in this section of the chapter, as we create a custom "Valentine's Day" Nozzle. I am going to take you through the creation of a stylized heart vector shape object, by using only four data points, which is extremely optimized, from a "data footprint" standpoint. If you doubt me, take a look at the HeartNozzle file size, which is an order of magnitude smaller than the Niki-based digital painting file sizes that we have been working with thus far.

The first step is to click a starting vertex, at the top center of the canvas, about 25% of the way down, as is shown in Figure 6-6, in the left-hand pane. Click the end of the line at the right side of the document, at the same level as your start point, and after you click do not release the mouse button but instead drag downward to create the Bézier spline curve as seen in Figure 6-6. Release your mouse (left button), and click your second point directly underneath your starting point, where you want a heart tip to be. Again without releasing your left mouse button, pull the spline tensioning handles so they create a tip for your heart, as shown on the right-hand pane in Figure 6-6.

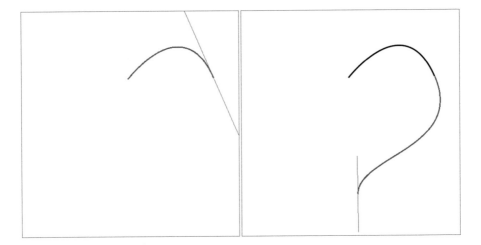

Figure 6-6. *Create first section of heart, then second section*

Next place the fourth vertex on the opposite side of the heart object, mirroring the second vertex placement, as seen in Figure 6-7 selected in red, and place the fifth point on top of the starting point, which will "close" the heart shape. Use the spline tensioning handles for each point to refine your curves, so that when you are finished, you have the nice stylized heart vector shape object that can be seen on the right-hand side in Figure 6-7.

Figure 6-7. *Refine Bézier Splines using Handles to Finish Heart*

Now that we have a foundational vector shape, we'll turn it into a raster object, make it solid, and make some variants, so that we have an Image Hose Nozzle that has some variation to it. We will start with rasterizing the shape, fill it, and drop shadow it to show you how these operations are done in Painter.

Creating a Solid Nozzle Image: Using the Fill Tool

Let's create a nice red color for your first HeartNozzle image. The first step, seen numbered as 1 in Figure 6-8, is to set your red color in the color wheel. I did this by clicking in the red paint in the Mixer palette. Next select the **Paint Bucket Fill** tool (#2) and click inside of the Heart in the canvas area. The **Commit** dialog (#3) will appear and asks you if you would like to commit your shape to an image layer. What this means is that you would be "rendering" your Heart shape vector data into a raster or pixel array type of data representation. Click Commit and then use the Effects ➤ Objects ➤ Create Drop Shadow menu sequence (#4), and accept the default settings (#5). Make sure to check the **Collapse to one layer** option, as you cannot nest layer groups, and we will be grouping your layered artwork later on during the work process. Click **OK** and create your drop shadow, to give your heart object a little bit of 3D height.

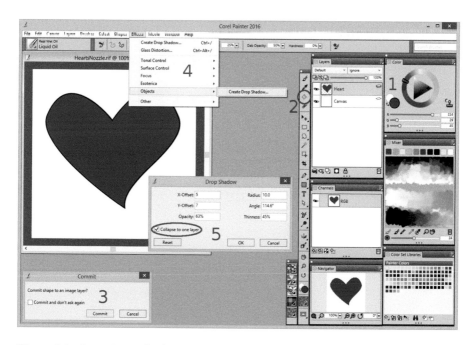

Figure 6-8. *Create Drop Shadow and Collapse to one layer option*

Right-click the **Heart and Shadow** layer, select **Duplicate Layer**, and then select your **Move Tool**, as shown in Figure 6-9.

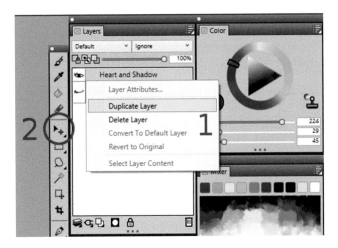

Figure 6-9. *Right-click to Duplicate Layer and select Move Tool*

Select the new layer and use the **Effects ➤ Tonal Control ➤ Adjust Colors** menu sequence, as shown in Figure 6-10, and set the **Hue Shift** to -5%, **Saturation** to **50%** and White **Value** to **75%**. This will create a nice pink heart color for the second Nozzle.

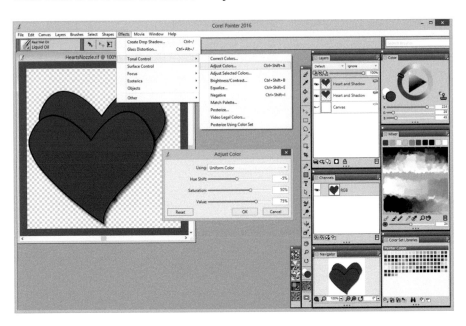

Figure 6-10. *Use Effects ➤ Tonal Control ➤ Adjust Color to Pink*

Next, let's add some slight rotation to this pink heart to differentiate it a little bit from the other hearts we will be creating for this Image Hose Nozzle.

Transforms in Painter: Using the Rotate Transform

To apply a rotational transformation to an object on a layer in Painter, select the layer, and use an **Edit ➤ Transform ➤ Rotate** menu sequence, as is seen on the left side in Figure 6-11. This will bring up the **Rotate Selection** dialog, shown in the middle of Figure 6-11. I used a value of negative **20** degrees, and then clicked the OK button to commit the transformation.

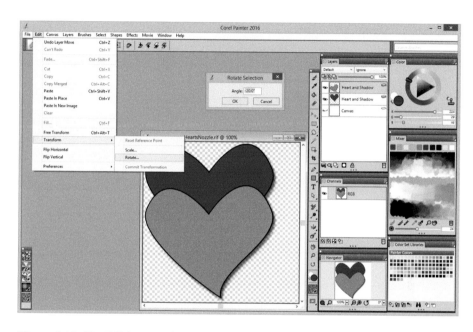

Figure 6-11. *Use Edit ➤ Transform ➤ Rotate to rotate Heart -20°*

Next, let's create a third heart object for this Nozzle, and this time we'll use a pattern fill, which you learned about in Chapter 4.

Select your original red heart layer, and right-click on it, and select **Duplicate Layer** a second time. Use the drop-down arrow on the Painter Assets Toolbar shown on the bottom left in Figure 6-11 (Painter calls this the Media Library, by the way), and select the Lotus Petals pattern, as seen in Figure 6-12, as we know that this pattern looks great inside of a heart object.

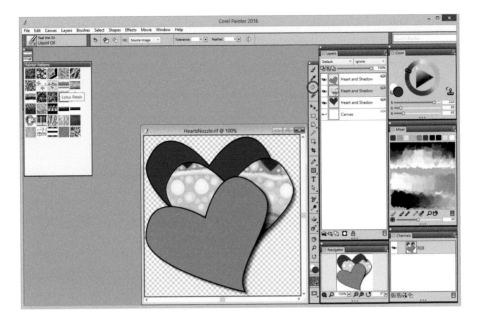

Figure 6-12. *Duplicate another Layer, and use Lotus Petals Fill*

Next select the Paint Bucket Fill tool, shown circled in red in Figure 6-12, and click in the middle heart, to fill it.

As you can see in Figure 6-12, we now have three hearts: one pink, one red, and one Lotus Flower; and all you have to do now is to rotate your Lotus Flower heart to differentiate it as well, and we will be ready to get into the Nozzle creation work process. This is getting exciting; soon, you will be using this Nozzle to spray hearts all over a photograph of your loved one!

Make sure the second layer is still selected, and use an **Edit ➤ Transform ➤ Rotate** menu sequence, as is seen on the left side in Figure 6-13.

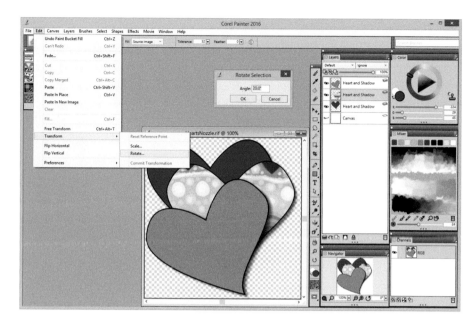

Figure 6-13. *Select Fill (Paint Can) tool; click inside heart*

This will again bring up your **Rotate Selection** dialog, shown in the middle of Figure 6-13. This time I used a value of positive **20** degrees, to rotate this third heart in the opposite direction, and then clicked on the **OK** button, to again commit the transformation, as can be seen in Figure 6-13.

Now all we have to do is to Group the Layers using the Layers ➤ Group Layers menu sequence, as shown in Figure 6-14, to show the Nozzle which graphics are part of the Nozzle definition.

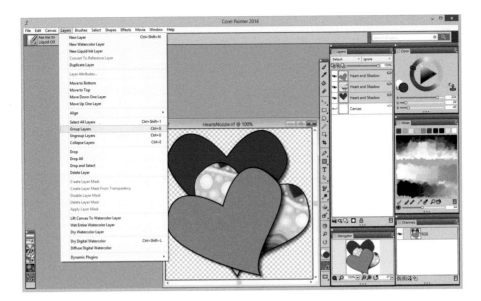

Figure 6-14. *Use Layers ➤ Group Layers and group the three heart layers together*

Creating a Nozzle: Group Layers and Make Nozzle

Now we have the Painter project foundation in place to create a Nozzle, including multiple layers, each with their own drop-shadowed object on them, we can take a look at the work process that is needed to create an Image Hose Nozzle. This involves a layer grouping step, and then a nozzle making step, and finally the adding of the newly created nozzle to the Nozzle library so that it can be selected from the Nozzles drop-down palette that we used in the beginning of the chapter to learn how Image Hose Nozzles are used.

As you can see in Figure 6-14, the hearts are now varied enough in both color and orientation, and they are on their own separate layers, so you can now turn these layers into a group because a Painter Nozzle uses a layer group to hold its element collection.

The work process for doing this involved selecting three layers at one time and then using a **Layers ➤ Group Layers** menu sequence to turn the multi-selected layers into a Group Layer.

The way that you multi-select layers is to select the first layer, and then hold down your **SHIFT** key and click the other two layers, all while keeping your SHIFT modifier key depressed.

Now that you have grouped your Nozzle artwork layers, you need to open the Media Library Panels using the **Window** menu and the **Media Panels** submenu. This submenu has five of its own submenus, as can be seen in the middle of Figure 6-15.

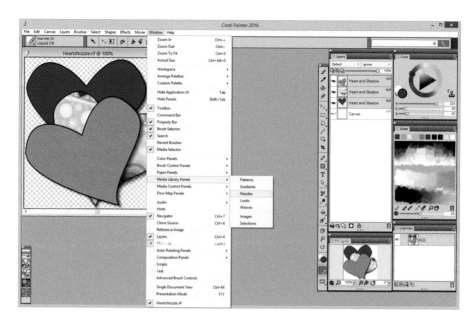

Figure 6-15. *Select the Window ➤ Media Library Panels ➤ Nozzles menu sequence*

Select your Nozzles submenu option, which will open the dialog that is shown in Figure 6-16, where we will complete the Nozzle creation operations of making the Nozzle, and adding it to your Nozzle Library so that it can be selected for use.

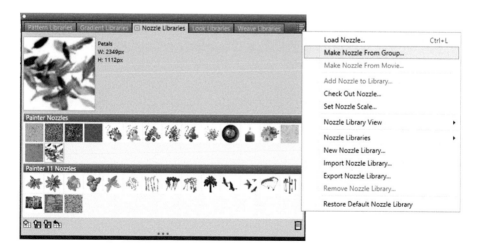

Figure 6-16. *Select the Make Nozzle From Group menu option*

Click the utilities drop-down menu on the right corner of the Media Library Palette, and select the **Make Nozzle From Group** option, as is shown in Figure 6-16. This will turn your image objects into an array of objects that the Image Hose can shoot out when the Nozzle you have just created is selected.

Once you use **Make Nozzle**, Painter can create an untitled RIFF which contains your Nozzle, as can be seen in Figure 6-17.

Figure 6-17. *Painter creates an Untitled Nozzle file for you*

Save the RIFF as HeartsHose.rif and use an **Add Nozzle to Library** option, seen in Figure 6-18, to add it to your library.

Figure 6-18. *Add the HeartsHose.riff Nozzle to your Library*

To test the new Nozzle, we have come full circle back to using an Image Hose and Nozzle. Open the Niki.png image, select the Brush Tool and the Image Hose Spray-Size-P Brush, and then paint a plethora of colorful hearts around the subject model in the photo image, as is shown in Figure 6-19.

Figure 6-19. *Select an Image Hose Brush and test the new Nozzle*

Now you have learned how to have Painter spray artwork on your canvas using a virtual airbrush, which streams any custom imagery onto your canvas, in any way that you want it to. Image Hose Nozzles are important tools to master for digital paintings and fairly simple to use, which is why we cover them early on in the book.

Summary

In this sixth chapter, we looked at how you can use the Image Hose and Nozzles to spray digital imagery onto your canvas and digital paintings in Painter. We looked at the work process for creating custom nozzles in case you want to create your own art in the form of Image Hose Nozzles for Corel Painter.

In the next chapter, you will take a look at **Quick Clone** and see how your digital photography can be manually painted on to the canvas to create customized digital paintings.

CHAPTER 7

■ ■ ■

The Mimicry of Digital Painting: Using Quick Clone

Now that we have covered the Image Hose and Nozzles that allow digital painting using raster image objects, the next most accessible way to create digital paintings in Painter is using the Quick Clone work process, which allows you to paint using color and location data culled from a digital photograph that you want to turn into a painting. Many analog (oil, pastel, acrylic, etc.) painters use this technique, painting from a photograph of the scene or portrait they wish to paint, so this is really a mimicry of the way that painters often work. The digital mimicry of pixel colors and location data also allows you to transmute the color, tone, and locale into brush strokes, allowing you to impart your creative genius onto the photograph you took, taking it to a new level by using digital painting.

During this chapter, we'll take a look at how to use the Painter **Quick Clone** feature, and we'll explore image adjustment features in Painter that can further enhance digital paintings.

Digital Painting with Photos: Quick Clone

There is more than one type of cloning operation in Painter 2016, but since I am progressing from the easiest work process to more advanced digital painting work processes, the next logical feature to cover is the Painter Quick Clone feature that allows you to paint over a photograph, turning it into a digital painting. This Quick Clone feature will allow you to prepare an image for digital painting in one simple step. Let's get started so we can begin having some fun! Open the Niki.png image using the **File ➤ Open** menu sequence, and then use a **File ➤ Quick Clone** menu sequence to set up your digital painting cloning document quickly, which is why this is called Quick Clone in the first place. Next, select the **Paper Textures** drop-down, using the arrow in the **Papers Icon** at the bottom of the Painter primary toolbar, as shown circled in red in Figure 7-1.

Figure 7-1. *Open Niki.png, use File ➤ Quick Clone, select Paper*

I selected a **Coarse Cotton Canvas** paper texture, which affects how the paint is applied to the canvas, simulating that type of paper as the surface of your digital painting canvas.

Once you invoke the Quick Clone canvas setup you can set how much of the image you are cloning from; in this case it's a Niki.png sample image I'm using for my new media book series. I decided on a setting of **85% canvas** to 15% image, so I'm not too distracted by the **source image** and can see what I am doing with the paint brush tool and effects on the resulting canvas image.

This is shown on the far-right side of Figure 7-2 in the **Clone Source** floating palette, which Painter opened up for you when you invoked Painter's Quick Clone digital painting engine.

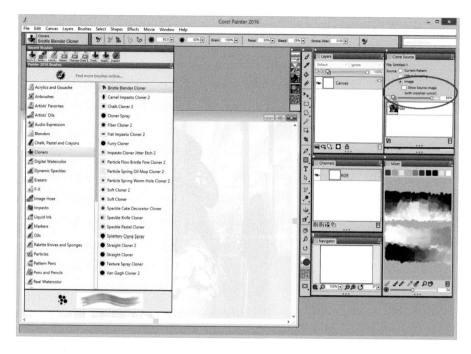

Figure 7-2. *Set Clone to 85% opacity, select a Bristle Blender Cloner Brush*

Next I selected a **Bristle Blender Cloner Brush** using the drop-down Painter
Brushes selector at the top left of Painter, as is shown in Figure 7-2. This brush will give
me some thick, coarse strokes with which I can paint in my background, which I will
later apply some special effects to toward the end of the chapter when I show you how to
enhance your brush strokes using digital image effects such as the ones that you find in
digital image compositing software packages such as Photoshop and GIMP.

Notice that when you invoke a Quick Clone scenario, that Painter will select a
Cloning Brush in your Painter Toolbar for you. It can be seen, selected in blue, in
Figures 7-2 and 7-3.

Figure 7-3. *Create Background Layer, Clone, Select Camel Impasto Cloner 2 Brush*

I used the **New Layer** icon, seen circled in red in Figure 7-3, to create a new layer that I named **Background**, as it will hold those brush strokes that will represent the background of your digital painting composition.

I am going to keep different parts of a digital painting on different layers so that I have more flexibility, not only in using different brushes but also in erasing selectively and applying different procedural effects later on during the work process. Leverage layers as much as you can in digital painting compositions as they allow you to do powerful things, as you will see over the course of this book (and have seen already).

I set the brush size to **16.0** pixels, seen set at the top left in Figure 7-3. I then painted in some of the background at the right third of the digital painting.

Now that I've painted in the right third of this digital painting, I am going to use a different brush to paint in finer detail for a white lace blouse in the left third of the digital painting. I will do this with the **Camel Impasto Cloner 2** Brush.

Before I add each digital painting element to my digital painting composition, I'll either invoke the **Layers ➤ New Layer** menu sequence or click the **New Layer icon** at the bottom of the Layers palette, seen circled in red, in Figure 7-3.

The next layer I will name **Blouse**, as I'm going to clone the blouse on the hanger in the source image by using the Camel Impasto Cloner 2 Brush that I selected from the Painter Brushes selector drop-down seen on the left-hand side in Figure 7-3.

You can see the Blouse Layer and the fine brush strokes I used in the left third of the digital painting in Figure 7-4.

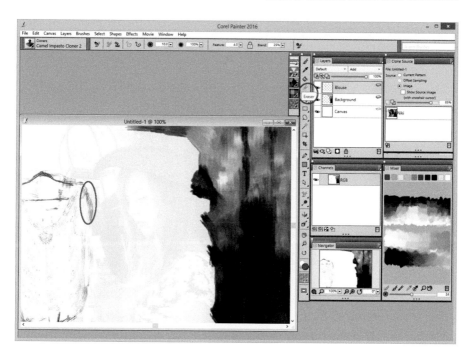

Figure 7-4. *Paint in Blouse on Blouse Layer, Select Eraser Tool*

One of the advantages of using layers becomes apparent when you have a need to erase something, such the errant stroke shown circled in a red oval on the left side of Figure 7-4.

To remove this, click on your **Eraser Tool**, shown circled in red in your primary Painter toolbar, and erase this portion, so that all you have on the Blouse Layer is **Camel Impasto** Brush strokes. Next we are going to create a **Model** Layer and paint in the face area for our model using the **Soft Cloner** brush and the **Clone Brush** tool. Do this by using the New Layer icon, as shown circled in red in Figure 7-3, and name the layer "Model" using a double-click on the layer name to bring up the editing field.

Select the **Soft Cloner Brush**, as is shown in Figure 7-5.

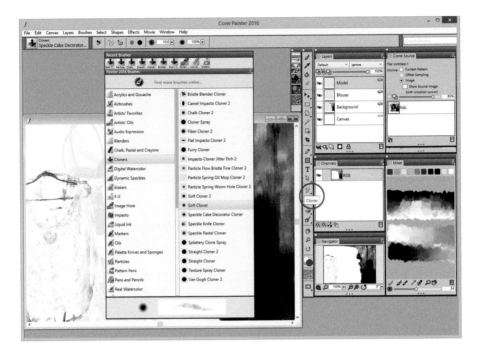

Figure 7-5. *Erase Paint on Blouse Layer, then Create a Model Layer, and then Select the Soft Cloner Brush*

Zoom into the face area of the model using the **Magnifier** Tool, shown circled in red, in your lower right-hand portion of Figure 7-6. Paint in her facial features, using the **Soft Cloner Brush**, as shown in the center of the canvas area.

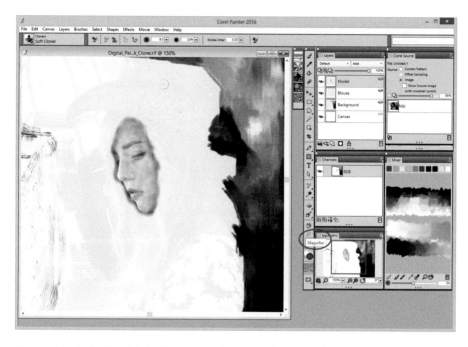

Figure 7-6. *Soft Clone Model Face on Model Layer after Magnify*

I drew the brush along the natural curves of the facial features, such as the bridge of the nose, the eyebrows, lips, eyelids, and eyelashes. The lighter areas can be gone over again to darken them, which I have done throughout the duration of the book, touching up the important facial areas, using the Model Layer. You will see this gradual progression, in Figures 7-9 through 7-14, throughout the rest of this chapter.

The next thing that I'm going to work on is the blue and yellow flowered shirt that this model is wearing, which should look great, using the correct cloner paint brush.

I selected the **Furry Cloner** Brush, which can be seen on the top left in the (closed) Painter Brushes selector shown in Figure 7-7. This is a really fun brush to use – so fun, in fact, that I also used it for the dark brown cowboy hat, which gives it a really cool look, as you will soon see.

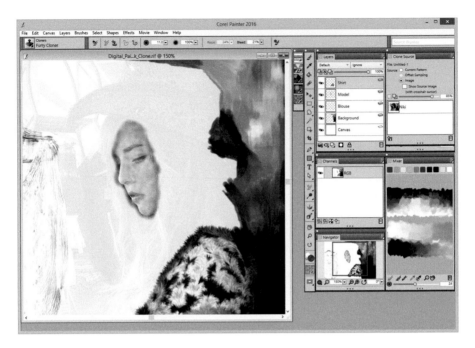

Figure 7-7. *Select FurryCloner Brush, Create Shirt Layer, Clone*

You can use short strokes to lay down "bursts" of flower like furry hairs, which will look really cool in bright colored areas of your digital painting composition.

Create a **Hat Layer**, as seen in Figure 7-8, and clone the hat using a **Furry Cloner** brush, following the edges of the hat.

Figure 7-8. *Create a Hat Layer and use the Furry Cloner for hat*

Finally, create a Hair Layer and again use a Soft Cloner Brush, since the hair is adjacent to the face, to paint in the model's hair, as can be seen on the canvas in Figure 7-9.

Figure 7-9. *Create a Hair Layer, and use a Soft Cloner for hair*

Notice that I've also finished filling in the background in Figure 7-9. One of the cool things about organizing your composition into layers is you can take a break from some areas by working on other areas of your composition. Another powerful aspect of layers is that you can isolate areas of a composition for application of special effects, color adjustments, contrast adjustments, blurring and sharpening operations, and the like.

This is done simply by selecting a layer containing that area of the digital painting that you want to process and then invoking that process, no pixel selection required. Layer order also controls which element is on top of, and underneath, other elements. This is also very important in digital painting image compositions, so master your layer operations and features.

Painting Effects: Enhanced Brush Strokes

Since we already covered tonal adjustment in Chapter 6, let's apply sharpening, special effects, and contrast optimizations in this section of the chapter. Select your Hat Layer, as shown in Figure 7-10, and use an **Effects ➤ Focus ➤ Sharpen** menu sequence to access a **Sharpen** dialog, where you can set seven parameters.

Figure 7-10. *Select Hat Layer and use Effects ➤ Focus ➤ Sharpen*

Use **Gaussian** Sharpening Aperture and an **Amount** of **30%**. Leave Highlights and Shadows at 100% (default) and deselect the Blue color channel, which will give the resulting brush strokes a warm color temperature as you'll see when you select **Preview**. The results of the Sharpen processing are shown in Figure 7-11.

Figure 7-11. *Hat is now more detailed; select Background Layer*

Next, let's select your Background layer, and make these brush strokes appear as though they are constructed with molten glass. Use an **Effects ➤ Focus ➤ Glass Distortion** menu sequence, seen in Figure 7-12, select **Preview**, and play with the options.

Figure 7-12. *Use the Effects ➤ Focus ➤ Glass Distortion filter on the Background layer*

The results of Glass Distortion are seen in Figure 7-13.

Figure 7-13. *Set Glass Distortion algorithm values with Preview*

Finally, let's enhance the contrast of that lace blouse, as it is kind of drab, and we can make those thin brush strokes "pop," by using the **Equalize** Tonal Control. Select your **Blouse** Layer, and then use the **Effects ➤ Tonal Control ➤ Equalize** menu sequence to open the **Equalize** dialog, as shown in Figure 7-14.

Figure 7-14. *Use Effects ➤ Tonal Control ➤ Equalize on the Blouse layer*

Select the Preview option and move the **Black Point** arrow slider to the right **25%** to increase the contrast. I also used a 60% setting for the Gamma Slider, to tweak the visual results I am getting in the blouse, which now shows all my paint strokes.

Summary

In this seventh chapter, we looked at how you can clone digital photography and use the pixel color data in the Painter Brush Engine so that your digital paint strokes that you place onto your canvas automatically match the color values of the source imagery. We looked at different cloner brush types, using layer operations to segregate (politically incorrect word, I know) an area you are working on, and how to apply effects to enhance the paint strokes later on by simply selecting these named layers.

In Chapter 8, you will take a look at **Image Effects;** since we already started looking at these in Chapter 6 and in this chapter, we might as well continue to explore the Effect menu and the power it allows you in refining the look and feel of your digital painting compositions.

CHAPTER 8

■ ■ ■

The Algorithms of Digital Painting: Plug-In Filters

Now that we have covered the Image Clone digital painting work process, including looking at a couple of the powerful digital image processing algorithms held in Painter's **Effects** menu that can enhance a digital painting workflow, the next logical thing for us to do, in this chapter, is to go ahead and look at some of the other digital image effects processing algorithms that Painter offers. These can be used on your digital imagery, if you don't own Photoshop, or on the digital painting that you are creating in Painter. It's up to you to use these algorithms creatively and innovatively within your workflow, and this will take some time and practice to achieve.

During this chapter, we'll take a look at how to use the Painter **Effects** menu and submenus. We will explore these image algorithms, which can be used on your digital photography or to further enhance your digital painting. We can't cover every one of these effects filters, also called "plug-ins" in some of the other software packages such as GIMP, but we will cover some of the more impressive ones, so this will be a fun chapter indeed!

Painter's Pixel Processing: Effects Menu

As you've seen, digital painting is a lot of work, most of which you do manually, hopefully using professional tablet and stylus hardware. There is, however, an area in Painter where algorithm effects can be called into play to process all of the pixels in the digital painting or in a layer in the composition, and all you have to do is sit back and watch the pixel processing being done for you. You can do things with these effects algorithms that would take you hours to do manually using the brush tools, so this should be an interesting chapter for you, as you can direct an image processing algorithm in Painter to produce any special effect result that you may want to see in your digital painting artwork, with a click of the mouse. Let's get started!

Embossing: Applying Surface Textures in Painter

Let's take a look at one of the powerful algorithms from the **Surface Control** Effects submenu first, as it can create some really powerful 3D special effects that can give your artwork a sense of depth. Open your **3dRenderedCar.png** digital image that comes with this book and select the **Effects ➤ Surface Control ➤ Apply Surface Texture** menu sequence, or if you have used this algorithm recently, the **Effects ➤ Apply Surface Texture** menu sequence, as shown on the left in Figure 8-1. The Apply Surface Texture dialog is shown on the far right, and as you can see I have selected the **3D Brush Strokes** texture and a **Softness** of **1**. I selected **Inverted** to make the surface texture come above the surface, and used a 100% **Amount** and 100% **Picture**. I used 0% for both **Shine** and **Reflection**, and a 1.2 **Brightness** setting and a 4 for **Concentration** of light, with a 1.41 **Exposure** value. I left **Light Color** as White, and I used the complex lighting algorithm (by not selecting **Simple lighting**) and 1 **Light** source. The only way to really experience what all of these settings will give you is to select the **Preview** check box and experiment with these sliders and settings. To apply this algorithmic effect, you can use the OK button. To try different embossing artwork on top of your image, use the square brush stroke drop-down menu at the top right of the dialog, next to the Using drop-down selector. I used the brush preset that features staffs of musical notes, as it looked really cool over the 3D car when I applied it, as you can see in the canvas area, shown in Figure 8-1.

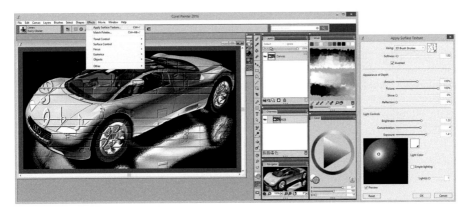

Figure 8-1. *Use Apply Surface Texture to 3D Bump Map your image*

Next, let's take a look at how to apply a color palette, taken from one image and algorithmically insert it as the color palette for a second image. This will essentially be impossible to do manually and thus would require this algorithm to do it for you mathematically, using pixel color values and locations.

Matching Color Palettes: The Tonal Control Menu

Next, let's take a close look at a couple of the powerful **Tonal Control** (submenu) Effects that Painter offers. The Match Palette algorithm applies the color and luminance of a source image to a target image, allowing you to perform professional film workflows such as color timing (color temperature matching across a series of images or frames), or matching the digital painting color look to a source painting or image. This Painter Effect requires two source images, allowing you to colorize one image using the color palette, or the colors used within, the second image. This can be useful for colorizing your digital painting brush strokes after they have been laid down. I will use our two source images here to show you more clearly what the algorithm is doing. Open the Niki.png source image in Painter, and place it at the bottom of the workspace, as I did in Figure 8-2. Next select the 3dRenderedCar canvas (window) since an active window will receive color palette data taken from your second inactive (unselected) window. Now you are ready to invoke the **Effects ➤ Tonal Control ➤ Match Palette** menu sequence, as shown in Figure 8-2, to access the Match Palette dialog, which contains a drop-down to select the palette **Source**; and five sliders, to control how a palette is applied using a Source, in this case Niki.png, to the Target, in this case 3dRenderCar.png, shown on the right in Figure 8-2.

Figure 8-2. *Applying the color of Niki.png to 3dRenderedCar.png*

I am using the **Color** slider to take the maximum colors from Niki.png, and display them in the 3dRenderedCar.png image. In this case, I want to use all of the color strength, or 100%, from the source image over the target image. You can "dim" this colorizing effect in the target image by using this slider, and for this reason you'll use this slider to fine-tune the effect.

I'm also applying a maximum 100% setting on the **Variance** value, which controls how many of the source colors are used in the target image, because I want to show you what the algorithm does, so I am applying all source color values to this target.

I am using a 33% **Brightness** slider value, which controls how luminance from the source image will affect a target image. I set **Variance** to 0% and **Amount** to 100% to show you the fullest extent of this palette mapping, from this source image onto the target image.

95

Next, let's take a look at another Tonal Control Effect, which allows you to **posterize** the image and control the number of colors that are used in your image. This is a popular effect that has even been utilized in popular television commercials.

Posterizing: Reducing the Colors Used in Artwork

Another useful Tonal Control effect is the **Posterize** effect, which allows you to specify the number of colors used in the color palette of the image that this algorithm is run on, that is, the image selected before the menu sequence is invoked. Undo any previous effects on the 3dRenderedCar image and select the **Effects ➤ Tonal Control ➤ Posterize** menu sequence as shown in Figure 8-3. I used a value of **7**, to show you can use only a handful of colors and still get a very reasonable image result.

Figure 8-3. *Reducing the number of colors used in the Car to 7*

Next let's take a look at another Surface Control Effect called **Sketch**, which allows you to turn an image into a sketch!

Sketching: Finding Edges in an Image with Painter

There is a really cool (and useful) Surface Control Effect that is called "Sketch," because it is an algorithm that finds edges in your image and turns it into a pencil sketch. We'll be using this a bit later on in the book when we look at another one of the Painter "workflows" but I wanted to cover it here as it is an often used special effect. To apply the effect to the Canvas, select the Canvas Layer, as shown in Figure 8-4, or create a New Layer to apply it on its own layer. You can also apply the effect to a selection area in your image. We will be covering Selection Sets and Alpha Channels in more detail in Chapter 9.

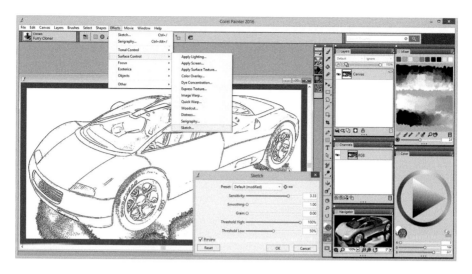

Figure 8-4. *Use the Sketch effect to turn imagery into sketches*

To get the cleanest lines in the sketch of the 3D Car, I set the **Smoothing** to the minimum value of 1.00 and the **Grain** to the minimum setting of zero. I used a **Threshold High** maximum of 100% and a **Threshold Low** of 50%. I also used the **Default Preset** at the top of this Sketch dialog as well. A plus and minus icon will allow you to save your own custom presets for future use.

I selected the **Preview** option to get a real-time preview of the results of these sliders as I dragged them, which is how I set the Preset Low to the 50% value. The last slider you will want to set is the **Sensitivity**, which will show you which image edges will become a part of your sketch.

I ended up setting the **3.33** value for Sensitivity, which gives me the high level of detail in this pencil and ink sketch result, which can be seen on the Canvas layer in Figure 8-4.

Next let's take a look at the often used **Sharpen Effect**.

Changing Focus: Color Sharpen Images in Painter

We looked at the **Sharpen** (Focus submenu) Effect in Chapter 7, as it related to making fine brush strokes, such as were used on the lace blouse, more pronounced (visible) to the viewer of your digital painting. Here we will look at its effect on the source image, and again at how useful the color-channel sharpen controls can be in providing an additional **tinting** effect in addition to the **focus sharpening** effect. Due to these seven settings in the Sharpen dialog, which is shown in Figure 8-5, this Focus effect can pull off a range of impressive tricks. To preview this effects algorithm again, **Undo** any previous effect, and use the Effects ➤ Focus ➤ Sharpen menu sequence.

Figure 8-5. *Adding Blue color tint, with a Sharpen Amount of 74*

I used a Sharpening **Amount** of **74** and left the **Highlight** and **Shadow** sliders at their maximum 100% default values. I then checked the **Preview** checkbox to see the results and tried color combinations of Red and Green (Yellow), Blue and Green (Cyan), Red and Blue (Magenta), and the colors individually.

Blue alone looked the best with the 3dRenderedCar image, so I used that for the screen shot, which can be seen in Figure 8-5. Sharpening also enhances the reflections, at the bottom of the 3D rendering, as well as the writing on the tires, interior detail elements, and the hubcaps.

Next, let's take a closer look at the **Esoterica** submenu of the Painter Effects menu, which has some really cool special effects algorithms. You can use the Esoterica effects to create a plethora of "commercially viable" special effects treatments.

Esoterica: Special Effects Using Painter Algorithms

The Painter Effects ➤ Esoterica submenu contains algorithms that will apply marbling and blobs, as well as creating custom tiles, grid paper, mosaics, polygon tessellation, mazes, and even Pop Art. There are also Growth and Highpass filters as well, as can be seen on the submenu in the middle of Figure 8-6. Custom Tile is a really useful filter for making your image into tiles or brick walls, which is what we are going to do with it, as is shown in the canvas area in Figure 8-6.

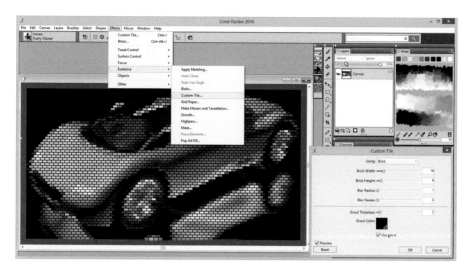

Figure 8-6. *The Custom Tile effect turns your image into bricks*

To achieve this effect I used the Custom Tile dialog and selected the Brick from the Using: drop-down selector menu, and specified an HDTV (16:9) aspect ratio for the bricks by setting the **Brick Width** value to 16, and the Brick Height value of 9.

I wanted the brick edge to be sharp and clean, so I left the Blur Radius set at a value of 1, and turned off the Blur by using a zero value for the number of Blur Passes.

To space out the brickwork a little bit, I used **2** pixels of **Grout Thickness**, instead of the default value of 1 pixel.

Since my source image has a black background, I left the **Grout Color** set to **Black**, as the Silver and Garnet color bricks look great against this background color, as you can see on the Canvas in Figure 8-6.

Next, let's take a look at the **Highpass** filter, which is a popular filter in digital audio editing, as you may have seen in my *Digital Audio Editing Fundamentals* (Apress, 2015) title. The filter allows you to make ethereal ghostly looking imagery.

High Pass Filter: An Audio Filter Works on Images

The Highpass filter algorithm can be accessed using the **Effects ➤ Esoterica ➤ Highpass** menu sequence, which can be seen on the top left in Figure 8-7. The algorithm filters out pixel values based on color, just like the Highpass audio algorithm filters out values based on soundwave frequency. This allows you to get a ghost-like effect. The Highpass dialog is fairly simple, with values for Amount of filtration and Aperture type (Gaussian or Circular). As you can see my 3D Car looks great as a ghost!

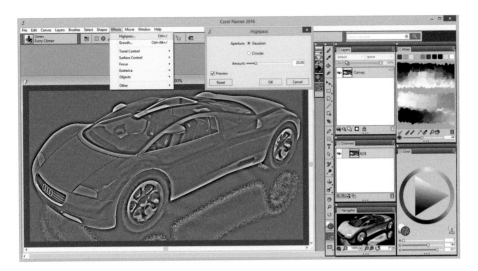

Figure 8-7. *The High Pass Effect turns your image into a ghost*

Next, let's take a look at another Esoterica algorithm, which is a lot of fun to use especially if you like comic books, printed artwork, or magnified printed artwork, known as Pop Art.

Creating Pop Art: Using the Pop Art Fill Algorithm

Finally, I am going to show you the fun-filled **Pop Art Fill** Esoterica Effects menu algorithm, which is accessed by using the Effects ➤ Esoterica ➤ Pop Art Fill menu sequence, as can be seen in Figure 8-8. I used the Image Luminance to create a Pop Art effect, as this image has a lot of dark and bright areas. I used a 33% Scale value to get a good side print or ink dot size and pumped up the Contrast value to a maximum 4 times or 400%. Finally, I matched the Black background color for the source image and picked a nice Orange color for a seasonal Halloween effect. The resulting image looks great. Make sure to explore the rest of Painter's Effects menu algorithms on your own time.

Figure 8-8. The Pop Art Fill Effect turns an image into Pop Art

Next, let's take a look at **SVG Filters** in Inkscape 0.91.

Inkscape and HTML5 Filters: SVG Filters

There is also a special effects menu in Inkscape, which is called the **Filters** menu, since most special effects are what are commonly known in the multimedia production industry as "Plug-In Filters." This is true for both Photoshop and GIMP, which you can explore further in the *Digital Image Compositing Fundamentals* title (Apress, 2015). What is really cool about the Inkscape effects, or filters, is that they are SVG Filters, and are also supported in HTML5, CSS3, and JavaScript, for all of you programmers out there. Let's explore these SVG Filters next. What this means is that you can do the exact same thing using code in HTML5 apps or web sites that you can in Inkscape. This means that every look and feel and special effect that you can generate in Inkscape on vector illustrations or digital imagery can be coded in CSS3 or JavaScript and invoked on any of your new media assets in your HTML5 applications, games, or web sites, and rendered on the client side, saving data transfer overhead and allowing you an order of magnitude of more special effects and even interactive special effects capabilities.

First, launch Inkscape, and create a 36 pixels thick, Red (224) color value, and four turns spiral object. This should be done by using the **Create spiral** tool, tool settings, and Stroke style and Stroke paint floating palettes. The resulting spiral, which should look like Ketchup squirted onto a Bun, can be seen in Figure 8-9. This is your vector object that we will be using to apply SVG Filter effects. It is important to note that these SVG Filter algorithms work on both vector and raster objects.

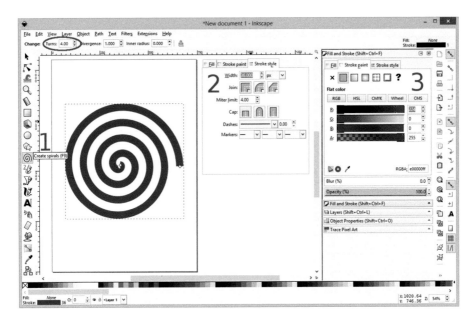

Figure 8-9. *Create a Spiral object 36 pixels wide, and set Stroke paint to Color Red 224*

First let's use a **Filters ➤ Bevels ➤ Bloom** menu sequence as seen in Figure 8-10 to create a shiny 3D look for the spiral object. The result can be seen on the right in Figure 8-10.

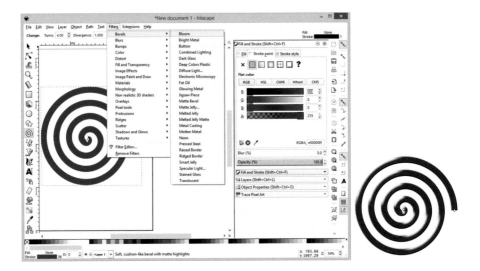

Figure 8-10. *Use Filters ➤ Bevels ➤ Bloom to create a 3D spiral*

Use an Edit ➤ Undo work process and a **Filters ➤ Shadows and Glows ➤ Drop Shadow** menu sequence, and apply the Drop Shadow filter next, using the Blur radius of 3 pixels and offsets of 6 pixels. The results for this Drop Shadow algorithmic processing can be seen in Figure 8-11, making the spiral float in the air.

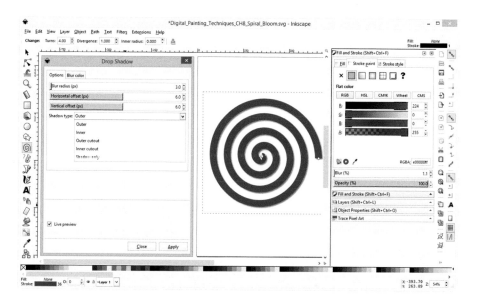

Figure 8-11. *Use Filters ➤ Shadows & Glows ➤ Drop Shadow filter*

You can explore the rest of the SVG Filters on your own time, as there is a lot more ground to cover in this book, regarding more complex topics such as alpha channels, layer-based compositing, brush dynamics, physics simulation, and more.

Summary

In this eighth chapter, we looked at how you can apply image adjustments and special effects on the pixel level by using the Painter Effects menu and the Inkscape Filters menu to implement algorithmic pixel-based effects processing. We looked at the different Effects submenus in Painter and applied some of the more popular image adjustments and special effects on raster source image assets, and then we did the same thing in Inkscape, only using vector source assets.

In Chapter 9 you will take a look at **Selection Sets** and **Alpha Channels** and learn how to leverage this amazing power that these capabilities afford to you within your digital painting composition creation work process and effect pipeline.

CHAPTER 9

■ ■ ■

The Selection of Digital Painting: Pulling Masks

Now that we have covered the Special Effect and Imaging Effect algorithms in Inkscape and Painter, let's get into some of the more technical aspects of layer-based digital compositing. Your selections, often called "selection sets" in the digital image, digital illustration, and digital painting industries are used to show the software where you want to apply pixel processing, and can be saved as "alpha channels" and used later on during the digital imaging, illustration, and painting production work process (workflow) as needed.

During this chapter, we'll take a look at how to use the Painter **Select** menu, as well as the Inkscape **Edit ➤ Select** submenu, and we will take a look at the basic selection operations for both software packages. We'll also take a look at the magic wand tool that allows selections to be created manually. If you are interested in covering selection sets and alpha channels in much greater detail, the *Digital Image Compositing Fundamentals* (Apress, 2015) covers this material in greater detail than this book does, as it focuses even more on the compositing pipeline.

Painter Selections: Algorithms or Wands

There are a couple of different ways to select things in digital imaging and digital painting software packages. You can use an **algorithm** to select things for you, based on things such as image luminance (black or white value), which can be useful for selecting clip media, for instance; or select things **manually** using something like the **Magic Wand** tool in Painter, Photoshop, or GIMP. We'll be looking at all of these work processes in the chapter, starting with the **Select** menu, which contains ways to select areas of an image algorithmically and then later on at the **Magic Wand** tool, which allows you to select areas manually. We will also look at how to save selections, as **alpha channels**.

Auto Selection: Having Algorithms Select Pixels

Again I am going to approach this chapter from the easiest to the most complex work process, so you can get to selecting pixels right away. The easiest way to select pixels in Painter is to have the software do it for you. There is a Select menu in Painter that has all of these functions organized under it, as can be seen on the left part of Figure 9-1. Select the Auto Select option, and in the dialog select **Using: Image Luminance**. This is the most often used way of auto selecting, based on the white or black values of the pixels in the image.

Figure 9-1. *A Select ➤ Auto Select menu sequence with Luminance*

As you can see in Figure 9-2, a selection is represented by tiny dashed lines. These are commonly called "marching ants" in the industry, because they also move so that they're visible to the content producer.

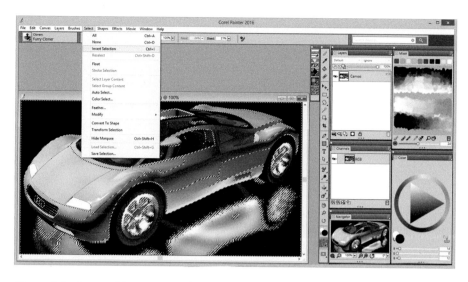

Figure 9-2. *Invert with an Invert Selection algorithm menu item*

Selecting What You Don't Want: Invert Selection

Next, let's take a look at one of the other most often used selection tools on the selection menu, the Invert Selection algorithm. This tool supports a workflow where you select what you don't want in your selection set, and then invert that selection. This tells the Invert Selection algorithm to "flip" your selection around to select everything that is not currently selected and to deselect everything that's selected. This is a popular workflow and is the reason for bluescreen or greenscreen sets, designed for using an Invert Select workflow.

To invert this selection, you will use a **Select ➤ Invert Selection** menu sequence, as is shown on the left in Figure 9-2.

Notice that the dark areas are selected in Figure 9-2 as indicated by the dashed line around the perimeter of the canvas on the outside of the black areas of the 3D Car image.

Once you have used the **Invert Selection** algorithm, these outer selection areas will disappear, as seen in Figure 9-3, to leave only the light areas selected; the car, and its reflection.

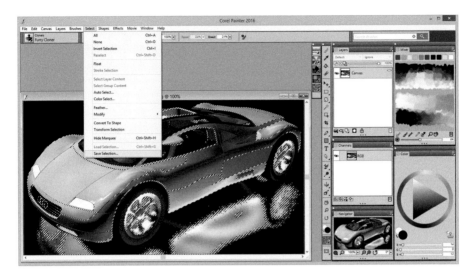

Figure 9-3. *Use Save Selection item and create an alpha channel*

Next, let's take a look at how to save a selection so it can be used any time during the work process. This is done using the Channels palette shown in the middle in Figures 9-1 and 9-2.

Saving Selections: Using Your Alpha Channels

There are a number of reasons to use a **Selection ➤ Save Selection** menu sequence, which can be seen on the left portion of Figure 9-3. The primary reason is, of course, to save finished selection sets for future usage as part of your project file. I use this work process in both digital image compositing as well as in digital painting software packages. There is another work process that involves using this menu sequence that's both more complex as well as more powerful. This is because once you save your selection as an alpha channel, it is turned into black and white (and the 254 levels of gray between these two colors). As any RGB color or alpha channel can be worked on using tools and algorithms, this means you can also edit or paint selections!

Let's take a look at how this works visually during the rest of the chapter, as how to create your selection set, which is also called "masking" in the multimedia production industry; it is an important workflow concept giving you significant power.

Use a Selection ➤ Save Selection menu sequence, and name your selection **AutoSelect-ImageLuminance** as seen in Figure 9-4.

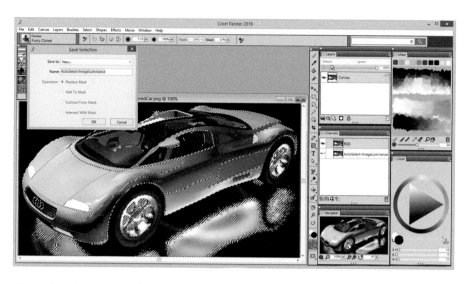

Figure 9-4. *Name your selection set AutoSelect-ImageLuminance*

Next, select the **AutoSelect-ImageLuminance** alpha channel using the Channels palette by clicking on it, as can be seen in Figure 9-5 in the right middle of the screenshot. In the Canvas area you will see the grayscale alpha channel data, which looks like a monochrome version of the image in this case, since you used the Auto Select algorithm to select pixels using luminance values, which as you can see, turns the image into a 256 levels of gray alpha channel data representation. While this is not so useful for selection purposes, it is useful for **layer masking**.

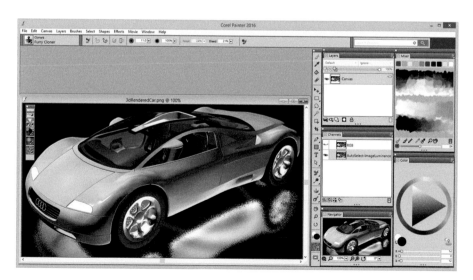

Figure 9-5. *Select the new selection using the Channels palette*

Layer masking, which we will be covering in Chapter 10, covering Layers; and why we covered masking and selection sets in this chapter first, allows the layers underneath the masked layer to "show through" the mask, onto the layer that's masked.

In this case, this will allow you to make an image under the current image layer look like it is being projected on that image, in the form of a 3D car. The layer compositing algorithm accomplishes this by using this alpha channel luminosity data.

Therefore for the purpose of creating this type of layer mask special effect, the **Select ➤ Auto Select ➤ Image Luminance** workflow, shown here, would be very useful in creating detailed alpha channel data, which can then be used in layer compositing special effects, and not for selection sets (masking objects).

Although algorithmic selection is a quick way to "pull a mask" as it is called in the industry, usually an alpha channel is generated manually, using the magic wand tool, which we will take a look at next, before we look at selections in Inkscape.

Manual Selection Sets: Using the Magic Wand Tool

To create a selection to mask out the car object and reflection you first select the **Magic Wand** tool, seen as #1 in Figure 9-6, and click in a **Black** area of the Canvas layer, seen as #2. Make sure that the **Canvas Layer** and **RGB Channel** are selected in their respective palettes. Next, use the **Select ➤ Save Selection** menu sequence, and specify **Save to: New** and then **Name** this selection **MagicWand-Select-Black**, seen as #3 in Figure 9-6.

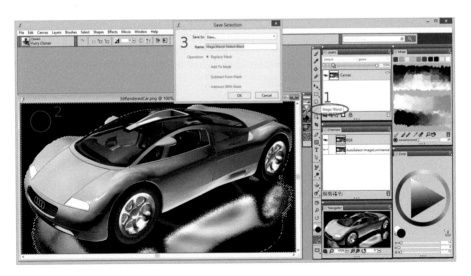

Figure 9-6. *Using the Magic Wand tool to select all black areas, and saving them using a channel*

As you can see in your Channels palette in Figure 9-7, a third channel, underneath the second alpha channel, will appear with the name you assigned to it.

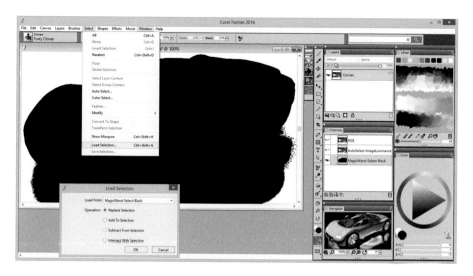

Figure 9-7. *To reload, select layer and Select ➤ Load Selection*

Since I have shown you the Select ➤ Save Selection work process, let's take a look at the **Select ➤ Load Selection** work process. Use the **Select ➤ None** menu sequence, which you can see in Figure 9-3, to deselect any current selection sets.

To load any selection that you have saved using an alpha channel, select the alpha channel (it will turn green), as seen in Figure 9-7, and use a Select ➤ Load Selection menu sequence, which will bring up the **Load Selection** dialog.

In your **Load From:** drop-down selector, choose the alpha channel that contains your selection set and the **Operation** you want the algorithm to use. This is usually a **Replace Selection**, but you can do **Boolean Operations** with selections in different alpha channels, by using these **Add To Selection**, **Subtract From Selection** and **Intersect With Selection** options. These options can be seen in the Load Selection dialog shown in Figure 9-7.

This feature can be used to allow complex selections and selections stored in more than one alpha channel.

Your loaded selection can be seen in Figure 9-8, and now you can use the **Invert Selection** menu item, and select your car and reflection instead of the black area that you selected with the Magic Wand. If you want you can save the inverted selection as **MagicWand-Select-White** by using the **Select ➤ Save Selection**.

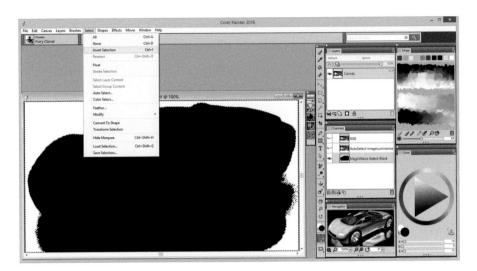

Figure 9-8. *Invert selection to instead select the subject area*

Now that the Car pixels are selected, use an **Edit ➤ Copy** menu sequence, as shown in Figure 9-9, and copy the Car pixels.

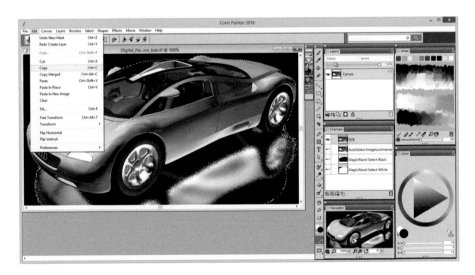

Figure 9-9. *Use Edit ➤ Copy to copy only the selected pixels*

Now that the selection set pixels are in your **clipboard**, which is an area of memory in your computer, you should use the **Edit ➤ Paste** menu sequence. This will automatically create your **Layer 1** in the Layers palette in the digital painting composite as is shown selected in green on the right side on Figure 9-10.

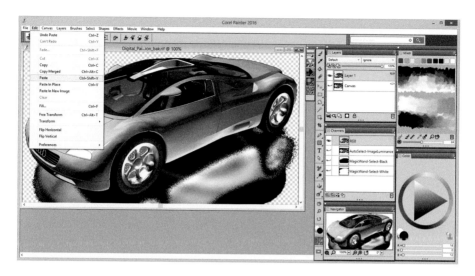

Figure 9-10. *Use Edit ➤ Paste to put selected pixels in a layer*

Now you can use the **Eraser** tool, seen selected in Figure 9-11, to refine your selected object. I decided to remove black areas underneath the reflection, as you can see in Figure 9-12.

Figure 9-11. *Use Eraser tool to paint out remaining black areas*

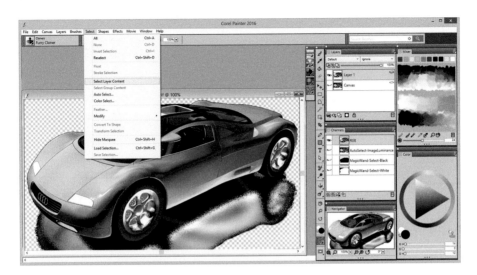

Figure 9-12. *Load finished selection using Select Layer Content*

Once you refine your object selection by using an Eraser tool, you can create a new selection, using the **Select ➤ Select Layer Content** menu sequence. You can then use the **Select ➤ Save Selection** to create an alpha channel to save the new selection.

You can use a **Transform Selection** algorithm to convert a Magic Wand (Pixel Array) selection to a Vector (Path) selection so that you can use your **Select ➤ Modify** (submenu) algorithms. This Select ➤ Transform Selection menu sequence can be seen on the left-hand side of Figure 9-13.

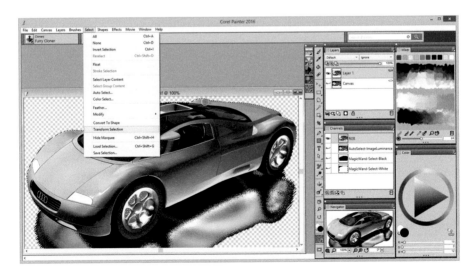

Figure 9-13. *The Transform Selection converts raster to vector*

Use a **Select ➤ Modify ➤ Contract** menu sequence to remove the one pixel wide black line around car. **Path Nodes** with **Selection Adjuster** tool are also seen circled in red in Figure 9-14. This tool can be used instead of the Transform Selection menu item.

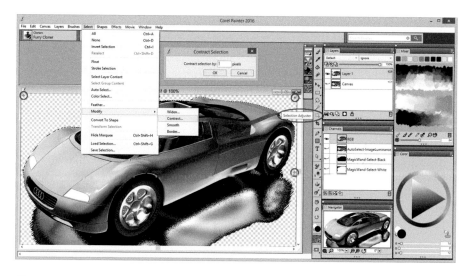

Figure 9-14. *Contract the selection by one pixel, to remove black line border around car*

Once you contract the selection by one pixel, use **Invert Selection**, to select only this one pixel wide black line, then use the **Edit ➤ Clear** menu sequence to remove this black border, and clean up the object mask. The results can be seen in Figure 9-15, and you now have a relatively clean masked 3D car object.

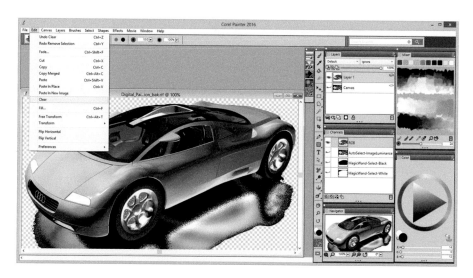

Figure 9-15. *The final masked car object has very clean borders, once selection is cleared*

Next, let's take a look at selections in Inkscape, which are under the **Edit** menu and don't have quite as many features, because these selection algorithms deal primarily with vectors, and not raster (pixel) selection operations, which are complex.

Inkscape Selections: Selecting Vectors

Now let's cover selections in Inkscape, since I am trying to cover both Painter and open source Inkscape in case readers do not want to purchase Painter. Launch Inkscape and open the file from Chapter 4 named **Digital_Painting_Techniques_CH4_Stroke.svg** as can be seen in Figure 9-16. Click the **Edit** menu so that you can see the **Selection** section of the menu and the **Select Same** submenu. I copied and pasted the heart object twice and changed the stroke paint color to red to show some of the selection operations in Inkscape and named this Chapter 9 file **Digital_Painting_Techniques_CH9_Multi-Select.svg** so that I can show you some of the Inkscape selection operations as well before concluding this chapter on selection set, alpha channel, and object masking fundamentals. Open this file now, and we'll take a look at some of Inkscape's selection algorithms next.

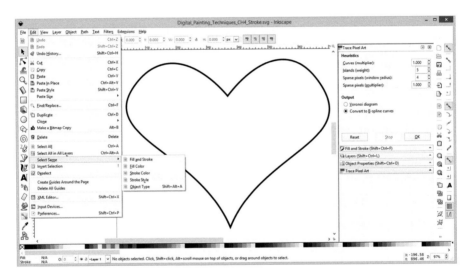

Figure 9-16. *Inkscape Selection uses the Edit ➤ Select submenu*

Use your **Arrow** selection tool, and select one of the red heart objects, as can be seen on the lower right-hand corner in Figure 9-17.

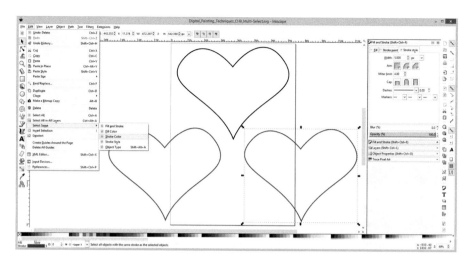

Figure 9-17. *Select red heart on right, and Edit* ➤ *Select Same* ➤ *Stroke Color*

Next, use your **Edit** ➤ **Select Same** ➤ **Stroke Color** menu sequence to invoke the multi-select algorithm. This Select Same submenu can be very useful, when you are building digital illustration projects using large numbers of **copied** objects.

It is important to note that **cloning** objects with Inkscape creates raster (bitmap) copies of your vector objects, so if you want vector copies use the copy ➤ paste work process.

The results of this selection algorithm's processing can be seen in Figure 9-18. If these objects had been cloned rather than copied, this multi-selection operation would not have been successful, as the algorithm looks for vector objects only.

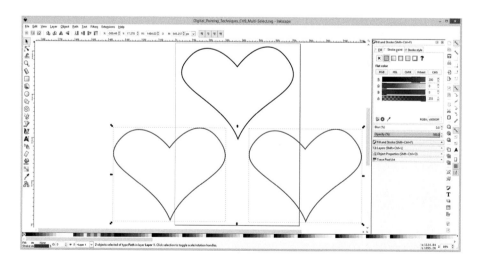

Figure 9-18. *Edit* ➤ *Select Same* ➤ *Stroke Color selection result*

117

Now that you have learned more about selecting and mask creation and alpha channel usage, we can proceed to take a look at the more complex topic of layers. Layers can contain what is called a "layer mask," and therefore Chapter 10 will build upon the knowledge from this chapter.

Summary

In this ninth chapter, we looked at how you can select pixels in Painter and vectors in Inkscape using selection algorithms and manual selection tools like Magic Wand in Painter and Arrow Select in Inkscape. We looked at how to save selections using alpha channels as well as how to restore them, and how to use editing tools to "pull a mask" and create custom selection sets to isolate objects and design elements in your digital painting compositing projects.

In Chapter 10 we will take a look at **Compositing Layers**, since we've already started looking at how to use these layers in several previous chapters already.

■ ■ ■

CHAPTER 10

The Compositing of Digital Painting: Using Layers

Now that we have covered selection sets, alpha channels, object masking, and similar operations that involve the use of layers and channels, it is time to look at more advanced layer functions in Painter, as well as layer functions in Inkscape, which are very similar to layer operations in digital image compositing software packages, such as Photoshop CS or GIMP. We have already covered creating new layers, naming layers, converting selected objects to layers, selecting layers, hiding and showing layers, and so on.

During this chapter, we'll take a look at how to use the Painter **Layers** menu and palette, as well as the Inkscape **Layers** palette and **Layer** menu, and learn about layer features in both.

Layer-based compositing is a complex topic, with Painter supporting dozens of layer features, and we will not be able to cover everything in one chapter. Indeed we have already covered some layer functionality already during other chapters and will continue to look at layer features in future chapters.

I cover compositing concepts in much greater detail in a *Digital Image Compositing Fundamentals* (Apress, 2015) title, if implementing complex image or painting compositing pipelines is an area that is of interest to you.

Painter Layers: The Compositing Pipeline

Compositing pipelines are found in almost every new media genre from digital audio editing (tracks) to 3D (the scene graph) to digital imagery compositing, digital illustration, and digital painting (layers). The reason for this is that complex projects and content production need to be "broken down" into component parts. This gives the producer far more control over individual elements in a composition, whether that is music, sound design, 3D, imaging, illustration, or painting.

For this reason, the first thing that I am going to show you how to do in this chapter is to break the 3dRenderedCar.png image down into component parts, with an entire 3D image on the Canvas (**backplate**, or bottom image), and only the car, and only its reflection, contained in different layers. We'll do this so we can digitally apply special effects, editing operations, and digital painting operations to specific areas within the image.

Composite Separation: Seamless Layer Elements

Let's start by launching Painter and using **File ➤ Open** to open a `Digital_Painting_Techniques_CH10_Layers_V1.rif` file. As you can see in Figure 10-1, I have created a layer containing just the 3D car, named **CarOnlyLayer**, on top of the Canvas layer containing the entire image. Select the Canvas layer, and use the **Select ➤ All** menu sequence to copy the image to the clipboard. Notice that just because you select a layer, you will not see what is in that layer unless you use the visibility (eye) icons for the layer to control what you are seeing in the canvas (work) area of the software package.

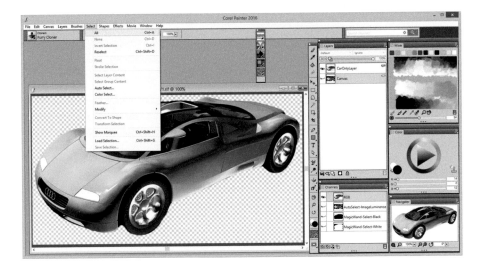

Figure 10-1. *Select Canvas layer, and use Select ➤ All to select*

The next step is to click on the **CarOnlyLayer** and select it so that it turns green, as is shown on the right, in Figure 10-2. Then use the **Edit ➤ Paste** menu sequence and create a layer above the CarOnlyLayer that contains the entire image pixels in it, so that we can extract the car portion later on in the work process. This is going to become your **ReflectionOnly** layer.

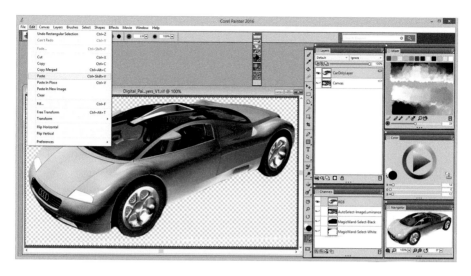

Figure 10-2. *Select CarOnlyLayer, and use Edit ➤ Paste to insert*

Name the new layer ReflectionOnly, as is shown in Figure 10-3. Next click on the
CarOnlyLayer to make sure it's selected. Painter is a "modal" software package, so
you'll need to select the layer that you want the algorithmic processing operation to be
performed on. In this case, this will be the **Select ➤ Select Layer Content** menu sequence,
as we want to select only the car, which as you can see is now selected in Figure 10-3.

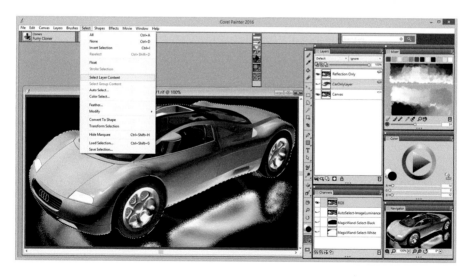

Figure 10-3. *Select CarOnlyLayer, and use Select Layer Content*

Before we remove the car from the ReflectionOnly layer's pixels, let's save a **CarOnlyMask** using a **Save Selection** dialog, as shown in Figure 10-4, so we have this mask for use later on.

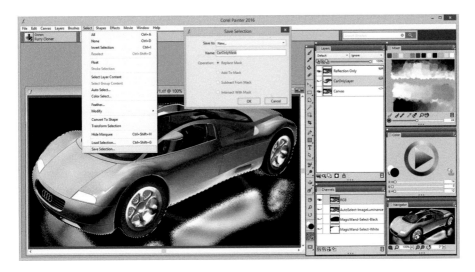

Figure 10-4. *Use Save Selection; name CarOnlyMask alpha channel*

Since Painter is modal, your next step is to select your **ReflectionOnly** layer so that you can use the CarOnlyMask, which you selected using your CarOnlyLayer, and delete these same car pixels with the **Edit ➤ Clear** menu sequence seen in Figure 10-5.

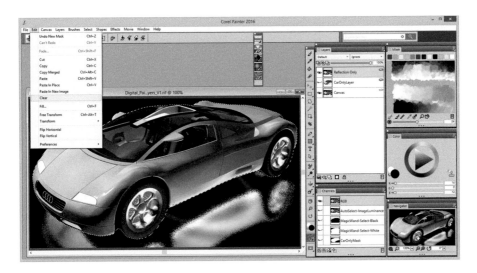

Figure 10-5. *Select ReflectionOnly layer, and use Edit ➤ Clear*

Finally, use the **Select ➤ None** menu sequence to deselect your active CarOnlyMask selection, as is shown in Figure 10-6.

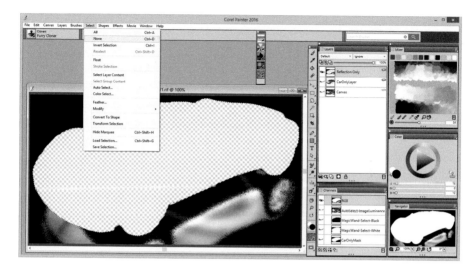

Figure 10-6. *Use Select ➤ None to deselect your selection*

Next, let's look at some of your basic layer operations.

Drag and Drop: Changing Composite Layer Order

The first thing you need to do is change your layer compositing order. Drag your ReflectionOnly layer (it becomes transparent), and drop it under the CarOnlyLayer, as is shown in Figure 10-7.

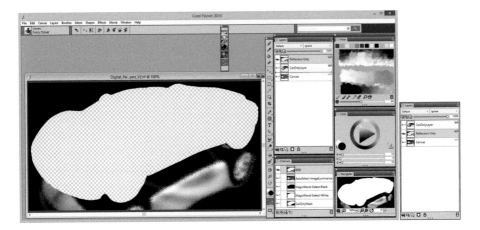

Figure 10-7. *Drag and Drop your ReflectionOnly layer under CarOnlyLayer*

Now that we have looked at reordering layers so that they composite (render) differently, like a stack of vellums, let's look at how to create duplicate layers. Right-click on the selected ReflectionOnly layer and select **Duplicate Layer**, as shown on the right in Figure 10-8, to create the duplicate.

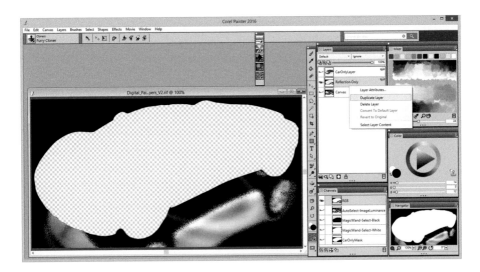

Figure 10-8. *Right-click on the layer, and use Duplicate Layer*

Let's look at Layer Attributes. Select **CarOnlyLayer** and right-click, and select **Layer Attributes**, shown in Figure 10-9.

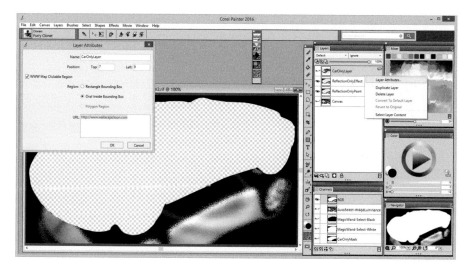

Figure 10-9. *Click the CarOnlyLayer, and select Layer Attributes*

In the Layer Attributes dialog, notice the Position gives you the 7 pixels (of black) at the top of your image, and the 9 pixels (of black) at the left of your image. This tells you the CarOnlyLayer needs to be positioned at X,Y location 9,7 to match up pixel for pixel with the other layers.

In order to show the **WWW Map Clickable Region** generation feature, I selected this option check box and used an **Oval Inside Bounding Box** selection; and finally, I entered a web site URL.

Also notice I have renamed the layers that we duplicated previously to be **ReflectionOnlyEffect** and **ReflectionOnlyPaint**, so that they match up with what we'll be doing with them later.

Also, notice in Figure 10-10 that I've used a **Layer Lock** feature, located at the bottom of your Layers floating palette, to lock the CarOnlyLayer so that you can't accidentally edit it later on. This is a useful layer feature that I wanted to cover before we get too far into this chapter. Next let's take a look at **Layer Masking**, so we can attach an alpha channel to each layer.

Layer Masks: Adding an Alpha Channel to a Layer

If you want to attach an alpha channel that is masking your object to your layer or turn the transparency you have created using the Eraser tool into an Alpha Channel and a **Layer Mask**, you should use the **Layers ➤ Create Layer Mask From Transparency** menu sequence, as is seen on the left side on Figure 10-10. You can also use the **Create Layer Mask** option right above this, and paint your layer mask from scratch, using Painter's edit tools.

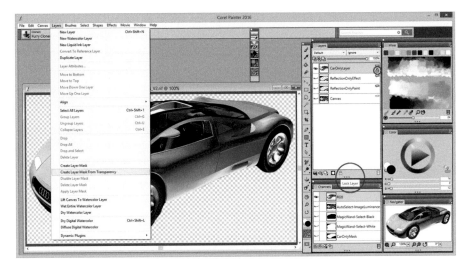

Figure 10-10. *Create LayerMask From Transparency (CarOnlyLayer), and Lock Layer*

Once you have created the layer mask for a layer it will be shown as a second layer icon, as shown in the selected layer in Figure 10-11. If you right-click on the layer mask icon, you will get the context-sensitive menu, shown on the right side of Figure 10-11, with the Layer Mask options.

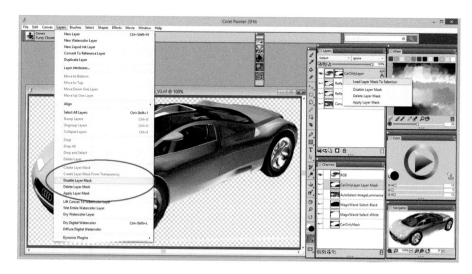

Figure 10-11. *Layer Mask options on Layers menu, and Right-Click Menu in Layers palette*

Also, notice on the Layers menu that once you create the Layer Mask you cannot create another layer mask for that layer, and the Create options are greyed out, and replaced by Disable, Delete, and Apply Layer Mask options.

Next, let's take a gander at Dynamic Plug-In Layers, apply a couple of these cool algorithms on the ReflectOnlyPaint layer, and create some cool special effects using these layers!

Dynamic Plug-In Layers: Special Effects Layers

Next, let's take a look at a special type of Layer that Painter offers called a **Dynamic Plugin Layer**. A Dynamic Plug-Ins submenu is located at the very bottom of your Layers menu and contains 10 impressive algorithms for applying special effects layers to your digital painting compositions. The first dynamic plug-in I want to show you is the liquid metal plug-in. This will allow you to paint on your layer using molten metal, with super cool results. Select your **ReflectionOnlyPaint** layer, and select the **Layers ➤ Dynamic Plugins ➤ Liquid Metal** menu item, as shown in Figure 10-12. This plug-in allows you to paint on your layer, using liquid metal in what looks a lot like molten metal paste.

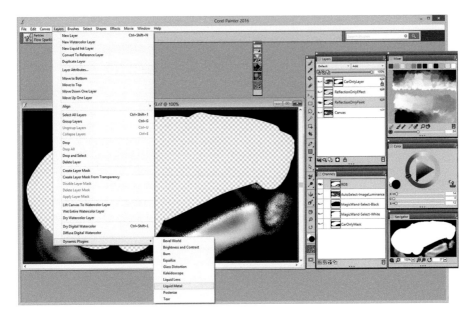

Figure 10-12. *Select ReflectionOnlyPaint layer and the Liquid Metal Dynamic Plugin*

A Liquid Metal dialog, shown on the right side in Figure 10-13, allows you to set the **Size**, **Spacing**, **Volume**, **Smoothness**, and **Rendering** characteristics such as a **Texture Map**, **Refraction** percentage, and **Amount** of texture mapping in the liquid metal. I selected the **Surface tension** option and painted a liquid metal border around the car's edge, as can be seen in Figure 10-13.

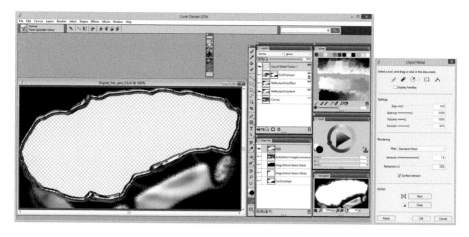

Figure 10-13. Paint the molten metal solder around the car edge

Next I selected the ReflectionOnlyEffect layer, as shown in Figure 10-14, and invoked a **Layers ➤ Dynamic Plugins ➤ Glass Distortion** menu sequence, to open up a **Glass Distortion Options** dialog, as seen on the top left in Figure 10-14. This algorithm applies as an effect and is not painted on the layer, so I set the **Preview** and **Inverted** options and selected an **Amount** of **2.0** and a **Variance** of **9**. As you can see in Figure 10-14, this gives me a much more impressive reflection result and smoothed metal effect around the car edges in this ReflectionOnlyEffect layer.

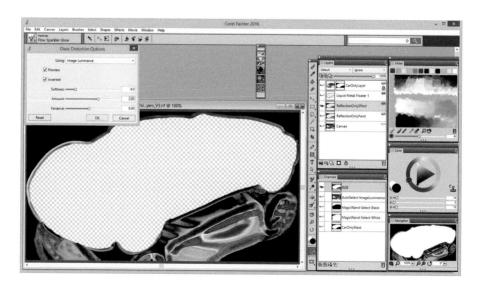

Figure 10-14. Applying Glass Distortion options to the ReflectionOnlyEffect layer

As you will see at the top right in Figure 10-14, I have dragged the CarOnlyLayer to the top position in the compositing layer stack, or pipeline if you prefer, so that all other layer elements are underneath the 3D Car part of the image. This will give the car a sharp, clean edge in the resulting composite.

Next I turned on the eye icon (layer visibility) for the CarOnlyLayer, so that the ReflectionOnlyEffect and CarOnlyLayer layers were showing at the same time, to see how the two layers work in conjunction with each other.

The result can be seen in Figure 10-15, and we're making steady progress toward creating a compelling digital painting composite image. The next thing I am going to do is to **colorize** the paint layer (ReflectionOnlyPaint) and then show you how to use "blending modes" to make the chromic reflection created by the glass distortion dynamic plug-in layer an order of magnitude more impressive. I am trying to cover as many of these advanced layer-based properties and features in this chapter as possible!

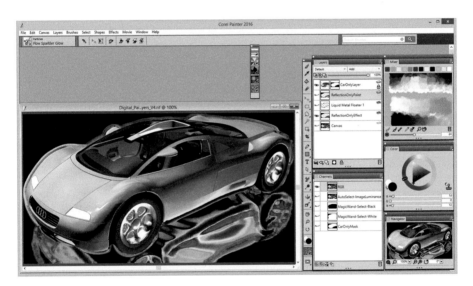

Figure 10-15. *ReflectionOnlyEffect and CarOnlyLayer are made visible using eye icons*

Next let's take a look at each layer's "blending modes, " or "composite methods," as they are called in Painter. Painter supports dozens of these pixel-math algorithms. Inkscape calls this collection of the four primary algorithms a "blend mode."

Layer Compositing Blend Modes: Color Algorithms

Whereas the **Opacity** slider at the top of the Layers palette simply controls a straight fade or "mix" between that layer and the layer composite that exists below it, the Painter **composite methods** (left drop-down), and **composite depth** (right drop-down) located above the Opacity slider, actually perform mathematics. These "Porter-Duff" algorithms take your color and alpha values into account in how each layer is **color blended** with the sum of the rest of the composite layers underneath it. What we are going to do next is to take the ReflectionOnlyPaint layer and "colorize" it, so we can paint your glass distortion reflection with it, creating an effect that is more than the sum of its parts. The first step in preparing this paint (color) layer is to select the ReflectionOnlyPaint layer, shown in Figure 10-16 and use the **Effects ➤ Surface Control ➤ Color Overlay** menu sequence to access the **Color Overlay** dialog. I used a nice gold color in the Use Color swatch selector and 75% Opacity blending to get a realistic golden wet rainwater effect for the layer. I used a **Paper** application template to get a bit more distortion in the wet area of the layer image and **Dye Concentration Mode**.

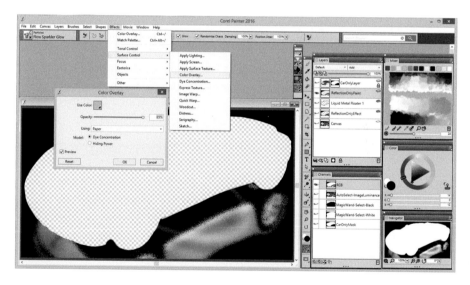

Figure 10-16. *Use the Color Overlay Surface Control Effect to create gold rainwater*

Next, set your left Composite Methods drop-down to use a **Hard Light** algorithm, as is shown in Figure 10-17. This applies an algorithm to the ReflectionOnlyPaint layer that applies its pixel color values to the silver composite below it, making the reflection into a stunning golden reflection of the car object. As you can see, Porter-Duff modes add plenty of artistic power!

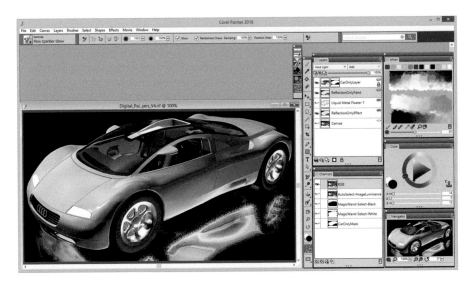

Figure 10-17. *Use the Hard Light Blending Mode to blend the two reflection effects together*

I created this image with a couple of the other blending modes as can be seen in Figure 10-18, so that you could see the different types of results you can get using Porter-Duff modes. Be sure to play around with these blending mode algorithms so you can learn how they will affect your compositing pipeline.

Figure 10-18. *The Screen and the Overlay Layer Blending Modes give different visual results*

Now that you have learned more about the selection and masking processes, and how these are used together with layers, alpha channels, and blending modes, you are probably starting to realize that using these more advanced work processes will give you more compositional power, artwork design, and content development flexibility.

Inkscape: Digital Illustration Compositing

Inkscape also has a Layers menu and palette, as you can see in Figure 10-19. Just like in other compositing software, you can right-click on a layer to access the layer features, or you can use the Layer menu. I used an **Add Layer** item to add the Layer 2 underneath Layer 1, so that I could show Inkscape's **blend mode**.

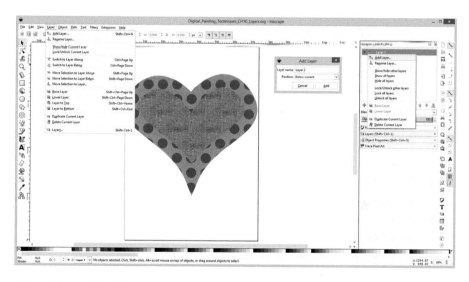

Figure 10-19. *The Inkscape 0.91 Layer menu and Layers palette*

Familiarize yourself with Inkscape's layer functionality as it works in the same way as Painter does, only with somewhat more limited functionality. I added the Niki.png image in Layer 2, as seen in Figure 10-20 and then set the Screen blend mode, shown on the right side at the bottom of the Layers palette, to show you how a vector illustration will blend with raster image assets. You can do the same types of effects in Inkscape using the SVG Filters and Blending Modes, which you can do in Painter, PaintShop Pro, CorelDRAW, GIMP, and Photoshop CS.

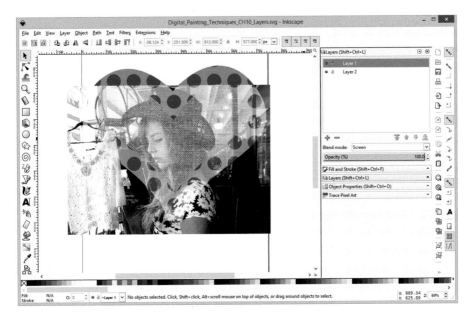

Figure 10-20. *Set the Screen blend mode for the vector artwork*

Summary

In this tenth chapter, we looked at how you can separate your digital painting projects into component layers, creating layer compositing stacks or pipelines. We looked at how to use layers for digital painting composites as well as how to reorder, lock, and duplicate them, as well as how to use specialized layers, such as Dynamic Plug-in layers, and how to combine layers with alpha channels using Layer Masks.

In Chapter 11, we will take a look at how to use Painter to do **Photograph Retouching**, since part of digital painting of portraits is preparing the subject for one of the digital paint workflows. After that, we can get back into more complex brush-based topics that Painter 2016 excels at and are more complex.

CHAPTER 11

■ ■ ■

The Refinement of Digital Painting: Photo-Retouching

Now that we have covered the foundational areas of selections, object masking, alpha channels, layers, and Porter-Duff blending modes in Inkscape and Painter, let's get into how to use some of the tools that are commonly found in the layer-based digital compositing software for both the digital image compositing as well as the digital painting genres. This process is commonly termed "photographic retouching" or **photo-retouching** for short.

During this chapter, we'll take a look at how to use the Painter **Rubber Stamp** tool, as well as the **Dodge** and **Burn** tools. These are your primary photo-retouching tools in Painter, other than the **Brush** tools, which can also be used for this purpose. The Rubber Stamp tool is called the Clone tool in Photoshop and GIMP, but since cloning is such an integral part of how Painter works, it is hidden in a pop-out icon (press and hold) with the Cloner Brush in Painter 2016. Underneath this icon are the Burn and Dodge tools, which are generally used with photo-retouching work processes, so we will look at these tools in this chapter.

Painter Photo-Retouching: Details Editing

All the tools in Painter can be used in photographic retouching workflows, including all of those we have covered thus far, and all of the brush workflows we have yet to cover. There are some specific tools that Painter has, kept in their own section of the primary Painter toolbar, which are specifically considered to be photo-retouching tools, especially in other digital image editing and compositing software packages such as Photoshop and GIMP. There are some image processing algorithms that Painter offers that can also be used in the work process, and so during this chapter we will remove some of the minor blemishes on your Niki.png practice image so that you can see how these tools can assist you in retouching photographs to remove blemishes.

Rubber Stamp: Sampling Pixels from Another Area

Let's launch Painter 2016 and open the Niki.png digital image. The first thing that I did was **zoom in 400%** so that I could see the areas of (slight) imperfection in the model's face, which is one of the primary areas where photo-retouching takes place. I detected a discoloration on the side of the nose and in the cheek area near the hairline (circled). Notice the **Navigator** floating palette on the bottom right in Figure 11-1 shows you the area that you are zoomed into, and has a number of zooming tools as well as Canvas rotation, which we will not be using in our photo-retouching workflow. I have also circled the Painter photo-retouching tools in red, in Figure 11-1, including the **Rubber Stamp** (selected) and the **Burn** (and Dodge) tool below it.

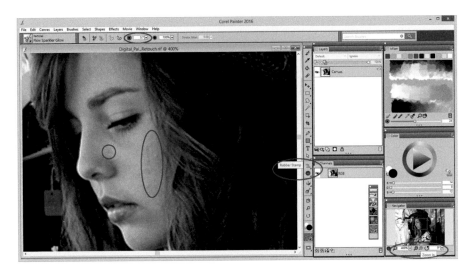

Figure 11-1. *Zoom in 400%, set your brush size to 3.7, and select your Rubber Stamp tool*

Let's start with that dark spot on the side of the nose and then deal with the larger more difficult cheek region. Your first step would be to zoom in even more; I zoomed in another 3 times to a 1200% zoom factor, as is seen in the image title bar, as well as in your Navigator palette, in the lower right corner of Figure 11-2. As you can see, the red active area editing box in the Navigator panel is smaller, showing you have zoomed in.

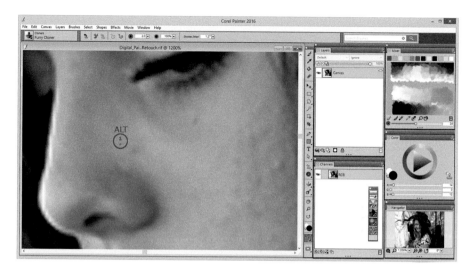

Figure 11-2. *Hold down ALT key, and click on an unblemished area on the model's nose*

You should use the zoom feature frequently during photo-retouching, so that you can see exactly what you are doing. The level of detail is very important to doing a great job removing any blemishes, which are often quite small, and sometimes hard to see. Zoom into the image, so you can view individual pixels.

Hold down the ALT key on your keyboard and click an area on the face that is clear, as seen in Figure 11-2. Painter will mark your source pixel with a green 1. Release the ALT key, and click the discolored area to replace it with the source pixels.

As you can see in Figure 11-3, this removes the blemish by replacing the darker pixels with lighter colored pixels that were located close by (next to) the target blemish you removed.

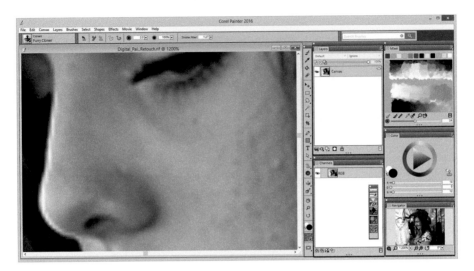

Figure 11-3. *The discolored area has now been eliminated using the Rubber Stamp tool*

Next, let's remove the dark area under the eye using the Dodge tool, another often-utilized photo-retouching tool.

The Dodge Tool: Lightening Underneath the Eye

Underneath the Rubber Stamp tool you will find the **Dodge** tool. If you don't see it, click and hold on the Burn tool, and when a fly-out appears, select the Dodge tool, which looks like a solid magnifying glass. This is seen circled in red in Figure 11-4, along with a **5 pixel Brush Size** setting at the top of the screen shot. I showed the brush in this screenshot as well, it is a thin gray circle under the eye, where I placed it, next to the area I would be working on, so that I could gauge what size to use for the Dodge tool.

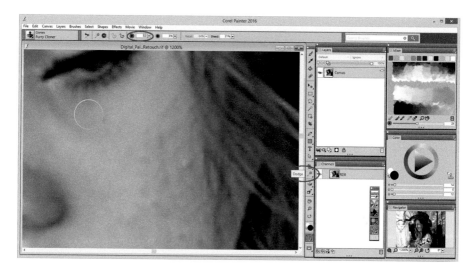

Figure 11-4. *Select the Dodge tool, and set a Brush Size of 5.0*

Next, I set the **Opacity** to a **2%** value, so the strokes of the tool had a more gradual lightening effect. Then I used some short strokes and clicks to deposit the lightening effect, and this removed the darker areas around the eye bit by bit.

This process will take some practice, so take some time, and work with this tool to get used to the gradual changes that this tool brings to your photographs and digital paintings. You really need good eyes and experience to see the gradual changes that the Dodge and the Burn tool bring to your digital imagery.

The result can be seen in Figure 11-5 along with the new Opacity settings, and the area under the eye looks revitalized.

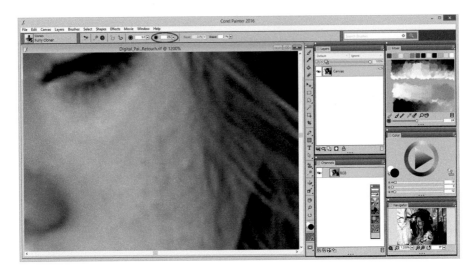

Figure 11-5. *Use a 2% Opacity and gradually paint out dark areas underneath the eye*

Next, let's darken the light areas in the lips using the Burn tool, another often-utilized photo-retouching tool, which darkens areas rather than lightening them.

The Burn Tool: Darkening the Whitened Lip Areas

Next, let's darken the red lips on the model in the photograph, by using the **Burn** tool. Click and hold your Dodge tool, located underneath the Rubber Stamp tool, and select the Burn tool. The icon for the Burn tool looks like a camera aperture. This is seen circled in red in Figure 11-6 along with the 2 pixel Brush Size setting, seen at the top of the screenshot. I again showed the brush in the screenshot as well; it is the thin gray circle on the bottom lip, where I placed it over one of the areas that I would be working on. Again, I did this so that I could gauge what size to use for the Burn tool. I used a 3% Opacity, which I later set to 2% as you will see in Figure 11-7, to control the amount of color burn (addition). Smaller percentages add less of the effect per stroke or click.

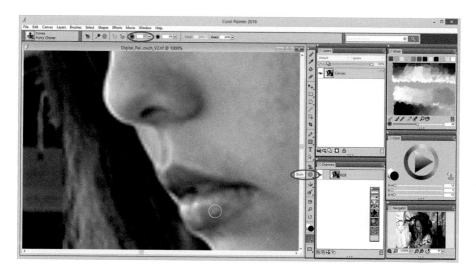

Figure 11-6. *Select the Burn tool, and set a 2 pixel brush size*

To apply the burning or darkening process, click on the light areas of the lip, specifically the bottom lip, to darken the lighter areas, using the hue (color) value present in that lighter version of the lip's color. Sometimes this works better than others, and in this case you will see that the color is a bit oversaturated, which we will fix later by using the Rubber Stamp tool.

As you can see in Figure 11-7, the light areas have been removed, but the color value is not blending into the lip areas as we would have liked, so we will need to use the **Rubber Stamp** tool and grab some color values that are nearby. This allows us to patch these areas up a bit, so that they look more natural. Photo-retouching often requires a combination of these tools.

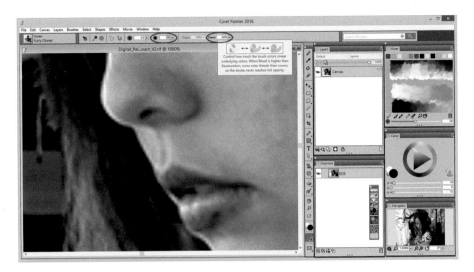

Figure 11-7. *Burn the light areas of the lips to increase the red value of those pixels*

Set the Rubber Stamp tool pixel size to 1 pixel and zoom in to the maximum allowed 1600%, as can be seen in Figure 11-8. Use the ALT key to sample a pink color next to the area you'll be working on, shown with a green 1, and click on the saturated areas to remove the visual anomaly that shows your retouching.

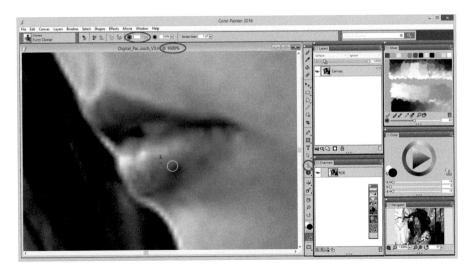

Figure 11-8. *Use the Rubber Stamp tool with a size of 1 pixel*

This will hide your saturated burn tool colors, as shown in Figure 11-9, and the lips now look fuller and more natural.

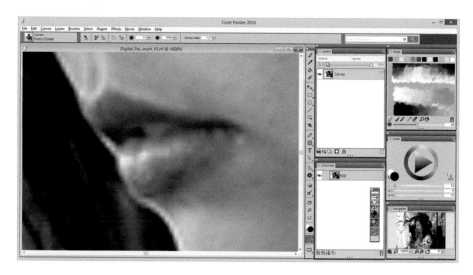

Figure 11-9. *Add some of the nearby pink lip color to cover those oversaturated red areas*

Now let's remove the blemish on the left cheek near the hairline, as can be seen inside of the brush, in the middle of Figure 11-10. As you can see, circled in red, I set the Rubber Stamp tool size to 2 pixels, which will just cover the blemish.

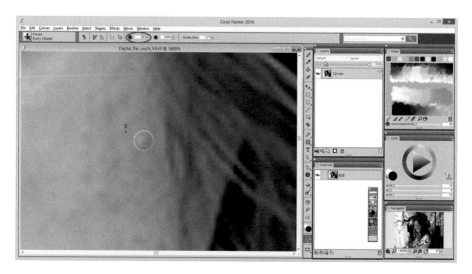

Figure 11-10. *Select 2 pixel Rubber Stamp tool to cover the blemish near the hair line*

As you can see in Figure 11-11, the blemish is now gone, and the cheek area looks much more natural with just one click.

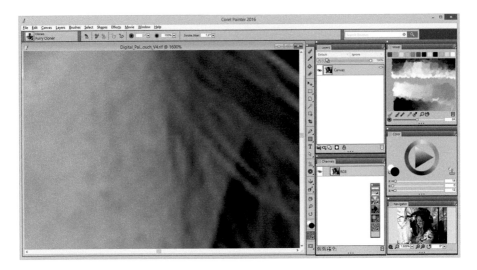

Figure 11-11. *Click on the blemish once or twice and remove it*

As you can see in Figure 11-12, the facial area is much improved. Practice using these photo-retouching tools on your own time. For instance, zoom into the cheek area, and continue to edit smaller anomalies, until this entire area is clean and unblemished. Use this as the photo-retouching work exercise for this chapter.

Figure 11-12. *This photo-retouched model looks much cleaner now*

Photo-retouching is an occupation in and of itself and takes skill, practice, time, and iteration to achieve pristine results.

Summary

In this eleventh chapter, we looked at how you can use digital painting software packages such as Corel Painter to do photo-retouching. If you are going to do this professionally, be sure to use an image editing software package such as GIMP, Corel PaintShop Pro, or Photoshop. I wanted to show you how to do this in Painter so you could prepare your photographs for cloning and learn about more of the core tools in Painter. We looked at how to use the Rubber Stamp to grab pixels from an area of your digital image or digital painting, as well as how to use the Dodge tool to lighten areas of an image and the Burn tool to darken areas of an image.

In Chapter 12, we'll take a look at Corel Painter 2016's **Sketching Workflow**, since we've already looked at how to create sketches using photographic imagery.

CHAPTER 12

■ ■ ■

The Coloring Book of Digital Painting: Sketching

Now that we have covered the related areas of photographic retouching of images, let's get back into the digital painting workflow used in Painter, one of which is a "sketch and paint" workflow. This workflow is a lot more common than you'd think. In animated films and television, there are artists who create the basic cel character outline and other "Ink & Paint" artists who fill that outline in with color and shading. This is also true in the comic book industry and probably in the casual game industry, both multibillion dollar industries.

During this chapter, we'll take a look at how to use the Painter **Sketch** algorithm, as well as more of the **Blending Modes** and **Layers**, so you get more familiar with using complex, layer-based compositing pipelines in your digital painting workflows. The workflow that we are going to follow during this chapter is what Painter calls a **Sketch** (or: Ink and Paint) workflow. There is also a sketch generator in Inkscape that works the same way.

A Painter Sketch Workflow: Coloring a Cel

The Painter Sketch workflow involves taking your digital photos and turning them into sketches (also called ink or cels in the industry) and then using layers to paint the different regions. We will use different inks and mediums during this chapter to show you some of those areas in Painter as well. We will also continue to look at advanced features, such as blending modes. I will start with the easiest workflow and progress to the more advanced workflows, as I have done throughout this book. First, we'll create a Sketch, using the Sketch Surface Control Effect, and then we'll use the original image we algorithmically culled the sketch from and have algorithms automatically paint it for us, by again using Painter blending modes. After that we will create layers and learn how to manually paint inside a sketch.

Automatic Sketch Painting: Overlay Blending Mode

Let's go ahead and launch Corel Painter 2016 and then open the `Digital_Painting_Techniques_CH12_Sketch.rif` project file. I have set this project composite up with a 3dRenderedCar.png image as the backplate (bottom) Canvas layer, as well as the Sketch layer so that you can algorithmically turn it into the sketch. The first thing that you need to do is to select the Sketch layer, as can be seen in Figure 12-1, and use the **Effects ➤ Surface Control ➤ Sketch** menu sequence to open the Sketch dialog. I again used a 3.33 Sensitivity and this time I set Smoothing to 1.8, and zero for the other three parameters. This will provide all of the primary lines that make up the car but won't include some of the detail lines, and some of the particle "noise" that comes along with using some of these other **Grain** and **Threshold** settings.

Figure 12-1. *Create a Sketch layer; apply the Effects ➤ Surface Control ➤ Sketch algorithm*

As you can see in Figure 12-2, this gives us a very nice-looking sketch to use for the rest of the work we are going to do in this chapter.

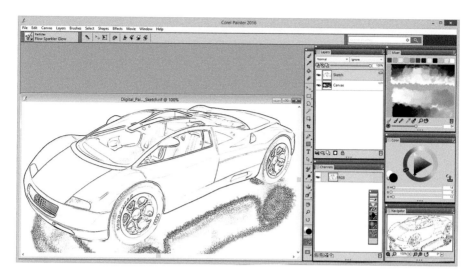

Figure 12-2. *Use the Normal blending mode to see only the Sketch layer*

To see this sketch without any blending modes, you would set your left **Composite Method** drop-down to: **Normal**. This means no blending modes will be applied, and is seen selected in blue in the upper-right portion of Figure 12-2, along with the black and white version of the sketch that you will be using for your "ink" outline that you will be painting in during the course of this chapter. First, I wanted to show you how to use an **Overlay** layer blending mode, which Painter calls a Composite Method, to paint your sketch for you using the image in the Canvas layer.

As you can see in Figure 12-3, when I select the **Overlay Composite Method** from the drop-down, as shown circled in red, a representation of the colors from this source image are blended into the sketch, creating an impressive result algorithmically.

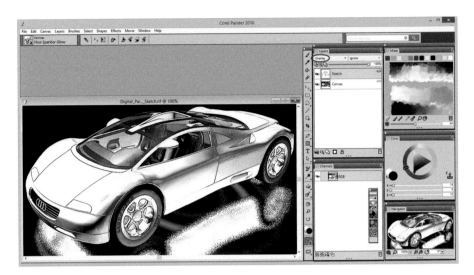

Figure 12-3. *Use the Overlay Blend Mode to color the Sketch layer using the Canvas layer*

Next, let's start adding layers and paint in the sketch!

Painting a Sketch: Painter's Natural Media Brushes

The next thing that we are going to do with this sketch is use different natural media brushes in Painter to paint in sections of this 3D Car. Some of these **natural media brush algorithms** in Painter require their own layers, specifically the **Watercolor** and **Liquid Ink** brushes. Since there is so much to cover in this digital painting software package, I'm going to cover these in the chapter along with a Sketch workflow so I can expose you to as many of the hundreds of features in Painter 2016 as I can. I will also show you **Chalk** and **Oil** Brushes later in this chapter.

Using Watercolor and Liquid Ink Layers: Algorithmic Brushing

I set the Sketch layer back to using a **Normal** blending mode and used the **Layers ➤ New Watercolor Layer** menu sequence to create a Watercolor Layer. Painter designated the layer as using a **Gel** Compositing Method, as can be seen circled in red in the middle of Figure 12-4. I also circled the **Layer Utility Menu** Icon, as you can see on the upper right of the Layers palette, and I put the **Layer Utilities Menu** on the right-hand side of the figure as well, so you can see its dozens of layer-related options.

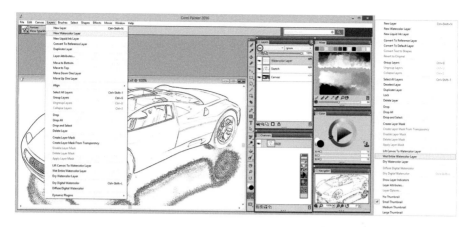

Figure 12-4. *Create a New Watercolor Layer, and designate the layer as being Wet*

I set a **Wet Entire Watercolor Layer** option by selecting this option, as shown in blue on the right side of Figure 12-4.

To match that wet pavement effect in the source image, I selected **Charcoal Paper** and **Sponge Grainy Wet** Watercolor Brush, as can be seen in Figure 12-5, from the Painter Toolbar's Paper Fly-Out and the Painter Brush Selector, respectively. You would turn this wet layer effect off by selecting your **Dry Watercolor Layer** menu option. This is shown on the right in Figure 12-6.

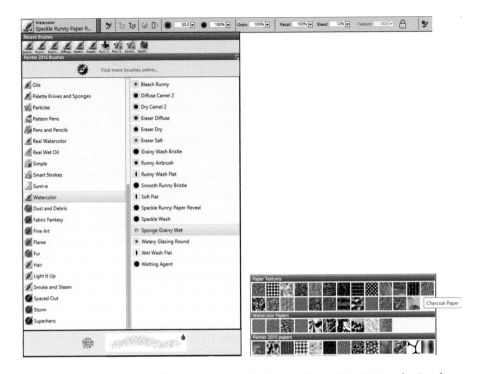

Figure 12-5. *Pick a Charcoal Paper texture and a Sponge Grainy Wet Watercolor Brush*

Paint some wet watercolor in the wheel reflection on the right of the image, as seen in Figure 12-6. The ink migrates on the layer surface, just like liquid will flow across a surface.

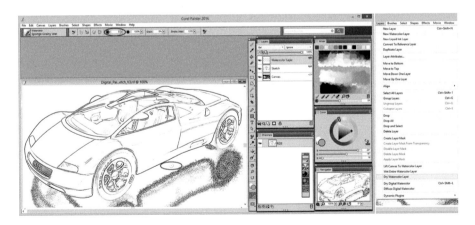

Figure 12-6. *Use wet watercolor brush to color in the reflection, then Dry Watercolor Layer*

To get more precise inking results, I turned off the wet effect using the **Layer ➤ Dry Watercolor Layer** menu sequence. As you can see in Figure 12-7, I then finished painting reflection areas at the bottom, and then I created a **New Liquid Ink Layer**.

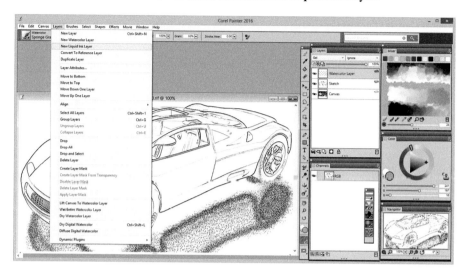

Figure 12-7. *Paint in the rest of the reflection, and then create a New Liquid Ink Layer*

Select a **Calligraphic Flat** brush, and use the Liquid Ink Layer dialog to set layer characteristics, seen in Figure 12-8.

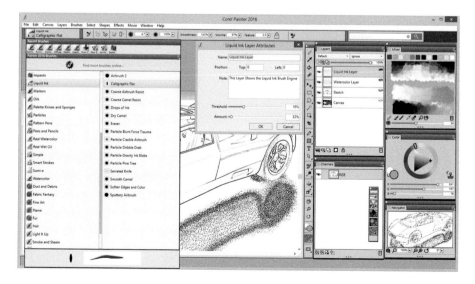

Figure 12-8. *Select a Calligraphic Flat Liquid Ink, then set the Liquid Ink Layer Attributes*

Select a **Wine** color, and paint in some of your car body, as shown in Figure 12-9. If you want to see the sketch's lines, you can select **Multiply Composite Method** to bring them through.

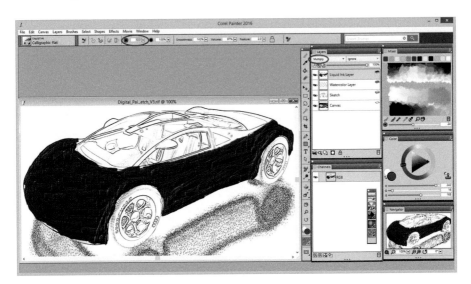

Figure 12-9. *Paint in some of the car with wine calligraphic ink and select Multiply blending*

Create a **New Layer**, name it **Chalk Layer**, select **Variable Width Chalk** as your brush, and a **Pink** color, as shown in Figure 12-10. Paint the hood of your car using transparent pink chalk. Notice I have turned off the visibility of the Liquid Ink Layer so you can see this better.

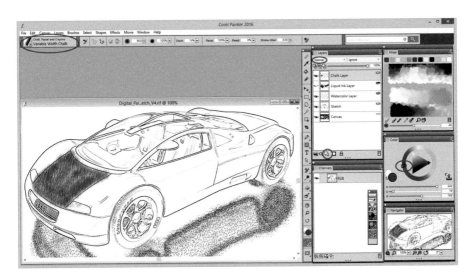

Figure 12-10. *Create a Chalk Layer; select a Variable Width Chalk, and color in the hood*

You can tell the chalk ink (brush) is transparent due to the fact that I have the **Normal Composite Method** set in the top of the Layers palette, as shown circled in red in Figure 12-10.

As you can see by now, if you're following along, trying to paint inside of these sketch lines, takes a bit of skill and practice, as well as the use of your **Eraser** tool, to clean up a bit. Next, I am going to show you how to "constrain" your brush strokes algorithmically using selections. These will be created with the magic wand tool so you can focus on your paint stroke characteristics and not where those strokes are going to fall.

Algorithmic Brush Placement: Selection Sets and Magic Wand

There is a way to tell Painter's brushes algorithmically where to apply paint to a layer, using a **selection set**, created using the **Magic Wand** tool. This works especially well using the sketch workflow, as you're selecting white areas constrained by black lines.

I created an **Oil Layer** to show the **Medium Bristle Oils** brush. Then I selected the **Sketch** layer and the **Magic Wand** tool, as is shown in Figure 12-11. In order to constrain my Oil painting to the front hood and fender, I used a low sensitivity setting of **8** for the Magic Wand, and I clicked in the middle of the hood, creating the selection set shown in the lower left.

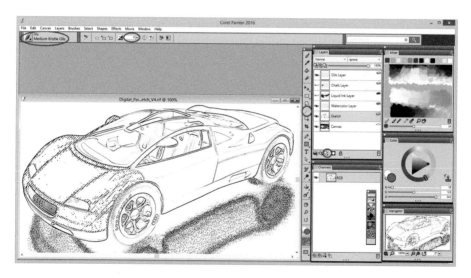

Figure 12-11. *Select the Sketch layer and Magic Wand tool; click on the hood area to select*

Next, select the **Oil Layer** and a **Blue** color; rename the layer Oil Layer Blue; select the Brush tool; and brush over the selection, which constrains the paint, as seen in Figure 12-12.

The selection set will constrain your paint strokes to only those selected areas, which is a very useful feature, as you can see.

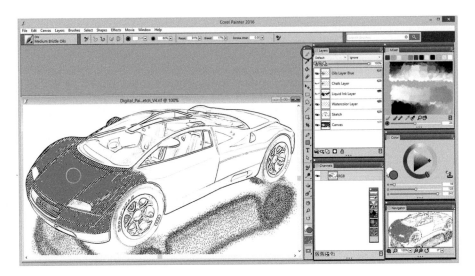

Figure 12-12. *Select the Medium Bristle Oils Brush tool, and paint over the hood selection*

Let's paint the rear of this car aquamarine, so create a new layer, named **Oil Layer Aqua**, as seen in Figure 12-13. Next, select the **Sketch** layer (remember modal operation) and select a **Magic Wand** tool and click in the rear area of the car. Use your color wheel selector to set an aquamarine color, as seen on the right-hand side of Figure 12-13, and select the **Oil Layer Aqua**.

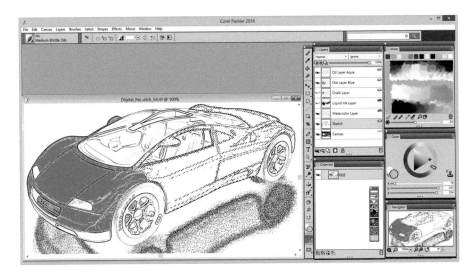

Figure 12-13. *Select the Sketch layer and the Magic Wand tool and select the rear of the car*

Modal operation requires that you select Oil Layer Aqua, as well as selecting your Brush tool, before painting over this selection set that was "culled" from the sketch layer earlier.

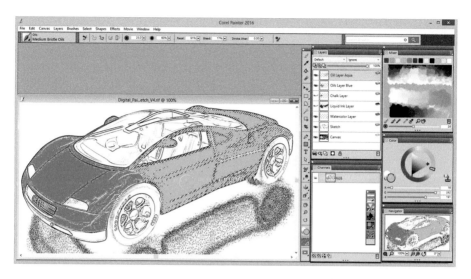

Figure 12-14. *Paint over the rear car selection set on the Oil Layer Aqua layer*

Next, use **Select ➤ None** to discard the selection set, so you can see the result. Select the **Sketch** layer, and select the **Soft Light Composite Method** to bring color up from the Canvas, as is shown in Figure 12-15. The results are quite visually enticing.

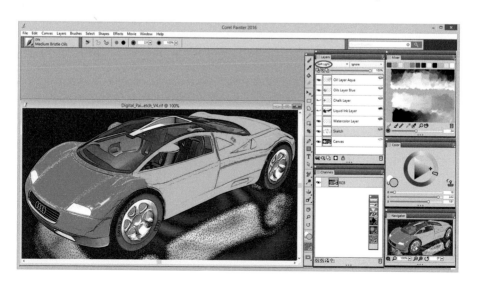

Figure 12-15. *Use Soft Layer Composite Method on Sketch layer to bring color from Canvas*

The result is pretty cool, using the interior of the car image to "paint" the interior of the sketch-based painting with the **Soft Light** blending mode algorithm.

Let's select Luminosity Composite Method as the blending mode algorithm next and see what this gives us. As you can see in Figure 12-16, Luminosity blending gives you a lighter color, thereby better illuminating the interior of the car. These colors match up better with the current painting pastel color look and feel.

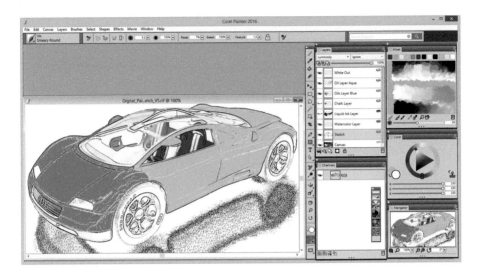

Figure 12-16. *Use a Luminosity Composite Method for a new look for the digital composite*

It should be evident by now of the composition flexibility that using layers gives you in creating the end result, as well as creating different versions of your digital painting, either for yourself or for your client.

There is also a sketch feature in Inkscape that works in much the same way called Trace Artwork that uses a **Potrace** open source software package as an Inkscape plug-in.

If you are interested in generating sketches in Inkscape as well, there is an entire chapter in the *Digital Illustration Fundamentals* title (Apress, 2015), which covers this subject in great detail using Inkscape 0.91.

Summary

In this twelfth chapter, we looked at one of Corel Painter's "workflows," the **Sketch Workflow**, as one way to proceed with a digital painting work process. We looked at how to use a source image and the **Effects ➤ Surface Control ➤ Sketch** algorithm to create a Sketch layer, above a source image layer. Then we used different types of Painter **Natural Media Brushes**, including the **Watercolor**, **Liquid Ink**, **Pastel** and **Oil** brushes, using the Paper Textures, to affect how the brush will be applied to the layer. We also looked at how to leverage layers and compositing methods, commonly called blending modes, to create digital painting compositions algorithmically. Let's continue leveraging these algorithms in Painter in the next chapter as well.

In Chapter 13, we'll take a look at Painter 2016 **Physics Based Brushes**, since we already looked at some of these brushes that simulate liquids moving on a surface during this chapter. We will look at some of the other algorithmic brushes, such as Particle Systems, Dynamic Speckle, and RealBristle brushes, during Chapter 13 as well.

CHAPTER 13

■ ■ ■

The Animation of Digital Painting: Physics Engines

Now that we have covered some more advanced brush types, such as the Watercolor and Liquid Ink brushes that use fluid dynamics physics algorithms to simulate real-world media, let's cover the rest of the physics-based brushes, including the particle system algorithmic brushes; and the audio sound wave algorithmic brush dynamics engine, called **Audio Expression**. The focus in this chapter is therefore animation, and, as difficult as this will be to portray in a static book with static images, you will just have to follow along with your trial version of Corel Painter 2016, unless you purchased it for your multimedia production software suite.

During this chapter, we'll take a look at how to use the Painter **Audio Expression** dynamics algorithm, as well as more of the **Particle System Based Brushes**, and how to work with **RealBristle** and **Dynamic Speckles** digital painting brushes.

Paint Stroke Attributes: Algorithm Control

There is one area that Corel Painter 2016 features that Inkscape will probably not have for quite some time, and that is the ability to have algorithms affect paint strokes based on external variables, including sound waves, or external real-time processing, such as applying fluid dynamics and particle systems dynamics to brush strokes as they occur, to simulate things such as liquid ink, watercolor, or even special effects. We will look at some of the more advanced algorithmic brush stroke types in this section of this chapter, using yet another one of Painter's workflows: starting with a blank canvas. This is the other major workflow used in Painter, other than a **Clone** workflow and a **Sketch** workflow, which we have already covered in the book. I'm going to look at a new feature of Painter 2016 first, Audio Expression; and then particle system features from Painter 2015, so we will cover the most recent features first.

Audio Expression: Your Digital Painting Vocoder

Start by launching Corel Painter 2016 and use a **File ➤ New** menu sequence to create a
NetBook (1024 by 600) resolution blank Canvas layer. Name the file Digital_Painting_
Techniques_CH13_Audio.rif and select a **Rough Charcoal Paper** and set a **Purple** color
using the Color Palette. The steps are seen numbered in red in Figure 13-1 and will set up
a Blank Canvas to test audio expression. Use **File ➤ New** (#1) to access the **New Image**
(#2) dialog, select the **Paper** icon (#3), and in the **Paper Textures** (#4) palette pick the
Rough Charcoal Paper option, and finally, set a **Purple** (#5) color using the Color palette
and its color spectrum picker.

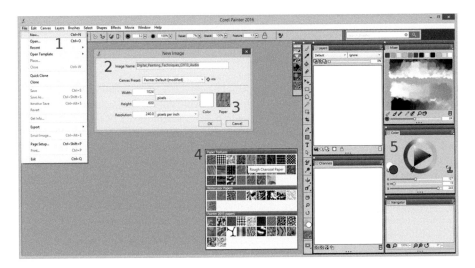

Figure 13-1. *Create a Blank Canvas; select Paper and Purple Ink*

Your next steps involve setting up, that is, activating, this Audio Expression engine
inside of Corel Painter 2016, and, after that, telling each Brush Strokes' characteristic that
you will want this real-time sound wave data coming into Painter to affect that particular
characteristic algorithmically, and how.

The first step, seen numbered in Figure 13-2, is to open the Audio Expression palette
inside your current user interface by using a **Window ➤ Audio ➤ Audio Settings Panel**
menu sequence.

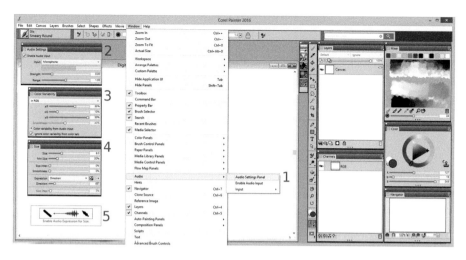

Figure 13-2. *Enable Audio Expression in an Audio Settings Panel*

The second step is to select **Enable Audio Input**, using a check box in the top left of this floating palette. A microphone will show the audio data using an **audio levels meter** underneath the **Input** drop-down selector, for which I specified **Microphone**. I left the **Strength** and **Range** sliders at the default settings.

Your third step is to open **Window ➤ Brush Control Panels** for each Brush Stroke characteristic that you want audio sound wave data to affect; in my case this was **Color Variability** and **Size**, shown as #3 and #4 in Figure 13-2.

Select the **Color Variability from Audio Input** and **Enable Audio Expression** options, as shown in Figure 13-2 as #3 and #5.

When you select these options you will get a **Using Audio Expression** dialog, as shown in Figure 13-3, telling you how to enable audio input and how to enable audio for Brush Controls.

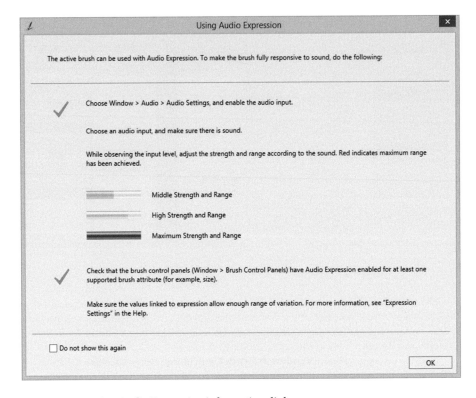

Figure 13-3. Using Audio Expression information dialog

Next I drew some lines from left to right while speaking into the microphone, as can be seen in Figure 13-4. These first and second lines were: Boom, Boom, Boom, Boom, and Bang, Bang, Bang, Bang (from CBS NCIS New Orleans and FOX Empire TV shows), and the third line was a sharp Ack, Ack, Ack, Ack, and finally, the fourth line was drawn in silence, as a baseline to show the difference. To get a more drastic result, you may want to use a synthesizer and controller to input more extreme sound waves for the Audio Expression engine to algorithmically process!

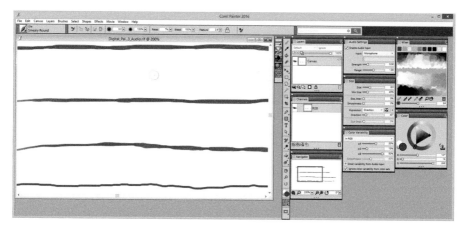

Figure 13-4. *Simple linear or flat brush strokes showing effect of audio input*

The Audio Expression engine feature of Painter 2016 will take some getting used to, and experimenting with, before being effective as part of your digital painting quiver.

A reason for this is because Painter's Audio Expressions are somewhat of a fringe, new wave feature, which no one really knows how to harness. However, it can open up a lot of creative avenues if you are willing to take the time to master it.

Particle Brushes: Animated Digital Paint Brushes

Painter's particle brushes harness the algorithms of physics in the area of particle dynamics (a precursor to fluid dynamics). The Brush emits the particles, which in turn paint your digital painting for you. As you might imagine this results in a unique look and feel for brushes that leverage the physics algorithms. The way that you control a particle brush to make it precise or chaotic is to adjust or "tweak" its particle system parameters. If you use the New Brushes Workspace Layout in Painter you will have all of the particle brush parameters at your disposal. The rest of this section will cover the different particle brushes.

Particle Brush User Interface: Arrange Position ➤ New Brushes

The first thing that we want to do before we start working with physics-based brushes, specifically particle systems brushes in this section of the chapter, is to change the Painter 2016 user interface design configuration to optimize our working area. We will need to accommodate some new and advanced floating palette UI elements that deal with hundreds of different options and characteristics. Integrating real-world physics algorithms with digital paint brush dynamics will create complex user interface elements in any software package, and Painter is no exception. The first step in creating a physics-based brush dynamics work environment, as can be seen in Figure 13-5, is to use the **Window ➤ Arrange Palette ➤ New Brushes** menu sequence.

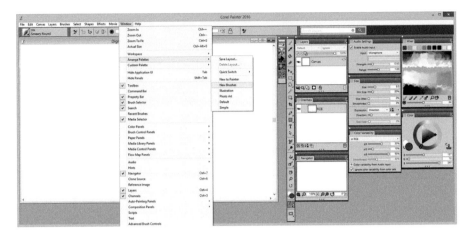

Figure 13-5. *Use a Window ➤ Arrange Palettes ➤ New Brushes menu*

Next, I am going to further modify this default Painter user interface configuration by removing the **Channels** palette, which we don't need in this chapter; and the **Mixer** palette, as we have the **Color** Picker Wheel. I will move your **Navigator** and the **Layers** palette into the right column with the Color palette and close the **Audio Settings** palette, as we have already looked at that functionality in the previous section of this chapter.

I'm going to keep the **Color Variability** palette, as this is useful for highly dynamic brush strokes that are provided by particles-based brushing. Color variability will yield far more realistic visual results, due to subtle variations in coloring.

Next, I used the **Window ➤ Brush Control Panels ➤ Gravity Particles** menu sequence to open the Common Particle palette for variables common to all particle systems-based brushes and the Gravity palette, since we are going to look at Gravity Particle Brushes in the next section of the chapter. Let's defy gravity!

Gravity Particle Brush: Stroke Velocity and Acceleration Factor

Gravity-influenced particle brushes are affected by the speed (velocity) of the brush stroke and how it accelerates and decelerates, as seen in Figure 13-6 in the "humps" in the Gravity Real Wet Oil brush stroke I drew across the screen. The more erratic and fast your brush stroke is with gravity brushes the more the paint stroke will vary from a normal natural media look and feel. As you can see I set a fairly high variation for color, especially Red (31%) and Blue (24%) and Color Smoothness (53%), which controls how quickly colors transition from one to another. The settings I chose using a brush color of Gold gives the camouflage color effect, shown on the canvas in Figure 13-6.

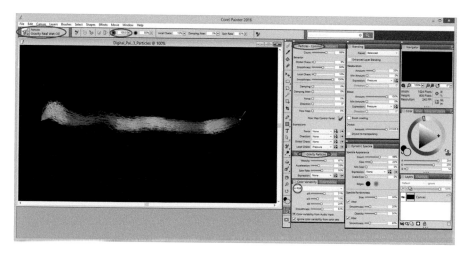

Figure 13-6. *Use Gravity Real Wet Oil Brush, and tweak your settings*

Gravity particle brushes use their own **Gravity Particles** palette, seen circled in red in Figure 13-6. Settings for three variables in the gravity brushes algorithm allow you to control the **Velocity** factor, an **Acceleration** factor, and a **Rate of Spin** factor. These settings allow you to specify a range, from 0% to 100% of how much you want these factors to influence the brush.

As you can see I set Velocity to **67%**, I set Acceleration to 33%, and I set Spin Rate to 50%. I did not set **Expression** as I am doing things using a mouse for this book for those readers who do not have the advantage of stylus or tablet hardware.

If you have stylus hardware, you can use this Expression drop-down to select what hardware data to attach these settings to. This gives you more control over how your digital painting hardware's data output controls the algorithm for this Gravity Particles floating palette and its settings. Be sure and play around with these settings to get a feel for what they'll do.

Flow Particle Brush: Liquid Effects Based on Fluid Dynamics

Flow particle brushes simulate flowing liquids using short-lived particles that "flow" out of the center of the brush "emitter" and are affected by the **Flow Map** for the brush stroke as well as randomized variables like **Chaos** and **Position Jitter**, as seen in Figure 13-7. Notice the way the fur-like threads are positioned in this **Flow Fur** brush stroke that I drew across the screen. As you can see, this time, I used **HSV** (Hue, Saturation, and Value) as the color model for the Color Variability palette, and I set a fairly low 12% variation for Hue (color temperature), and a medium 36% variation for color Saturation, and zero variation for color value (white versus black level, or luminosity). I used a 30% value for Color Smoothness to get a more pronounced transition from one green shade into another. The settings I chose using a brush color of Army Green gives an undersea foliage color effect, as can be seen in Figure 13-7.

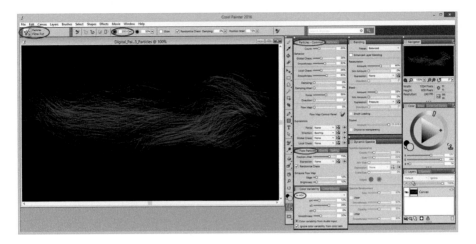

Figure 13-7. *Use a Flow Fur Brush Variant, and tweak your settings*

Flow particle brushes use a **Flow Particles** palette, seen circled in red in Figure 13-7. Settings for three variables for the flow brushes algorithm allow you to control **Position Jitter** and select an option to **Randomize Chaos**. You can also choose to **Enhance** the **Flow Map Edge** and **Brightness** settings from 0% up to 100%, and can use the Expression drop-down to tie any of these to data characteristics of the stylus and tablet, such as Tilt, Pressure, Bearing, Rotation, Wheel, Direction, or even Random.

As you can see, I set Position Jitter to 75%, I selected Randomize Chaos, and I set Flow Map Edge Enhancement to 10% and Flow Map Brightness Enhancement to 10%. I didn't set Expression as I am doing things using just the mouse to cover all readers.

Spring Particle Brush: Multiple Interconnected Spring Brush Tips

Spring particle brushes simulate webs of spring-connected brush tip particles, which "attach" back to the center of the spring brush "emitter." You can select a **center** (spider), **perimeter** (loop), or **matrix** (web) spring tip configuration and run length for the springs that interconnect the brush tip nodes, as shown in Figure 13-8 in the Spring Particles palette. Other **Behavior** settings include the **Stiffness** of the connecting springs, a **Jitter** factor for the stiffness setting, and a **Minimum Length** for the springs. As you can see, this time, I used **From Color Set** as the color model for the Color Variability palette, and I set a 50% value for Color Smoothness to get a more gradual transition from one color palette value into another.

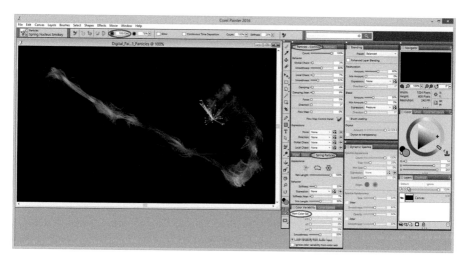

Figure 13-8. *Use Spring Nucleus Smokey Brush Variant, and tweak your settings*

You can also choose to assign any of the Spring particle variables using the Expression drop-down to tie any of these to data characteristics of your stylus and tablet, including Tilt, Pressure, Bearing, Rotation, Wheel, Direction, or even Random.

As you can see, I used a spider-legs configuration, with the maximum 100% Ran Length and fairly low 25% spring stiffness setting. I used the 50% Minimum Length setting, with a very low 7% Jitter for applying some random variation to my Stiffness. I didn't set Expression as I am doing things using just the mouse to cover all readers.

As you can see at the end of the brush stroke in Figure 13-8, you can actually see the Spring Particle Brush Tips, and this makes this brush the most difficult to master as even the slightest variation in how the brush is used changes the tips.

Dynamic Speckle Options: Fattening Your Strokes

Dynamic Speckle is a palette filled with options that you can apply to any type of brush, although these attributes are best used with Particle-based brushes, which is why we are covering this now; and with **RealBristle** brushes, which are digital paint brushes that simulate natural paintbrush bristles digitally. I selected a Real Bristle Soft Cover brush in Figure 13-9 to show you some of the Dynamic Speckle palette features, using an aqua color. The brush, palette, and color selection are shown circled in red in Figure 13-9, as well as a brush stroke enhanced using these dynamic speckle engine settings.

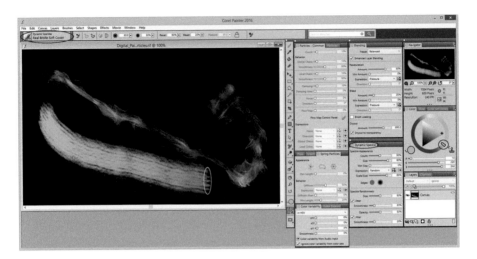

Figure 13-9. *Use the Dynamic Speckle palette to speckle brushes*

As you can see, I set the Dynamic Speckle **Count** to 50%, I set Dynamic Speckle **Size** to 90%, and I set **Minimum Size** to 0%. I set **Expression** to Random, as this does not require hardware, and I am doing things using a mouse during this book for those readers who don't have the advantage of tablet+stylus hardware.

If you have stylus hardware, you can use this Expression drop-down to select other hardware data to attach your settings to. This gives you more control over how your digital painting hardware's data output controls the algorithm for this Dynamic Speckle floating palette and its many settings.

I also set the **Scale/Size** setting to 85% to get a thick paint result; and crisp edges, as indicated by the blue circle with no blurred edges. I set 50% **Speckle Randomness Size** and I selected the **Jitter** option and set a 20% **Smoothness** factor. I used 50% for the **Opacity** setting and 20% Smoothness and again selected the Jitter option to provide more realistic strokes.

RealBristle: Simulating Natural Media Brushes

RealBristle is a Corel Painter technology that uses algorithms to simulate natural media brushes, that is, real paintbrushes, for your digital painting workflow. As you might have guessed, there is also a RealBristle palette, accessed using the **Window ➤ Brush Control Panels ➤ RealBristle** menu sequence, as shown in Figure 13-10; so open that now, so you can explore RealBristle.

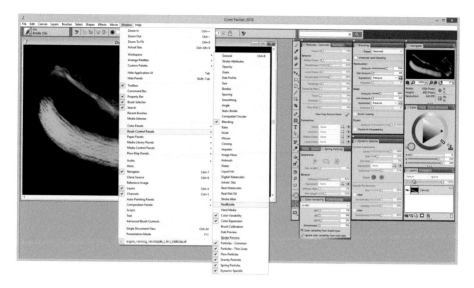

Figure 13-10. *Open the RealBristle Brush Control Panel in Painter*

As you'll see in Figure 13-11, to access the RealBristle algorithm, you'll first need to place a check mark in the **Enable RealBristle** check box.

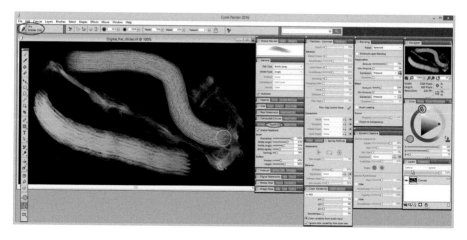

Figure 13-11. *Set RealBristle parameters to configure the brush*

I set the RealBristle **Brush Roundness** to **100%** and I set the **Brush Bristle Length** to 4.00. Next, I set the **Brush Profile Length** to 54% and the **Brush Bristle Rigidity** to 33%. I wanted the brush fairly pointed, so I set the **Brush Fanning** percentage to 16%. Larger Brush Fanning percentages allow the brush to fan out as pressure is placed on the brush tip, just like it will do in real-life usage.

Next, I set the Surface Friction and Surface Height for the RealBristle Brush Stroke, at 40% Friction and 60% Height. I then selected an orange color to differentiate the brush stroke from the other strokes. As you can see in Figure 13-11, bristles in this orange brush stroke are very distinguished and clearly defined. Like the other parameters in this chapter, you need to experiment with each of them to get familiar with that they do.

At the end of the day, there is no free lunch where your digital paint brush design is concerned, as you have started to see here, and will continue to see in the next chapter. With so many different parameters, all working in conjunction with each other, there is an almost infinite number of different digital painting brush strokes, looks, designs, and techniques that you can develop and utilize in your digital painting workflows. The only way to master this Corel Painter 2016 software is to spend the time experimenting with it, and ultimately, utilizing it to create digital paintings for your multimedia content pipelines.

Summary

In this thirteenth chapter, we looked at Corel Painter 2016 algorithmic brushes, especially those that used advanced algorithms such as physics, particle systems, fluid dynamics, speckle dynamics, and natural bristle brushing dynamics. These brushes use complicated mathematics and code to turn data from your tablet and stylus hardware into natural media brush stroke characteristics. We looked at dynamic brushes such as the Gravity, Flow, Spring, Speckle, and RealBristle brushes that use particle or physics algorithms to provide digital painting professionals with some of the most spectacular digital paint capabilities to be found in the world today.

In Chapter 14, we will take a look at Painter 2016 **Brush Characteristics and Design** since we have already looked at many of Painter's brushes during the book. After that we'll get into coding, scripting, and publishing topics to finish up the book.

CHAPTER 14

■ ■ ■

The Customization of Digital Painting: Brush Design

Now that we have covered advanced brush types that are provided in the Painter Brushes drop-down in the upper-left part of the Painter user interface, let's take a look at how you would create your own brush presets by using the dozens of brush attribute palettes available in Painter on the Window menu.

In this chapter, you will learn how to customize Painter **Brush Attribute Palettes** to create your own **Brush Variants**. The chapter will therefore be about getting more familiar with your different brush attribute palettes and the different parameters that are supported by Corel Painter's complex brushing engine, or, brushing algorithm, if you prefer that term. Either way you look at it, in the end, it all comes down to math and physics!

Brush Customization: Learn All Attributes

If you really want to create paint brushes as impressive as the ones that Corel Painter developers have created for the presets in the Painter Brushes drop-down selector, you'll have to learn all of the attributes, or parameters, that the brushing engine processes to make any given Painter Brush Variant function. As you know already, these brushes are grouped by brush type, and so you don't have to create brush variants from scratch, you'll usually just "tweak" brush variant parameters to create your own custom brush variants. Painter has more than two dozen, or more than three dozen, if you install the Brush Packs brush categories, many of which we've used during this book thus far. I will try to cover as many of the ones we have not looked at during this chapter on Brushes, but I could do an entire book on this topic, so you may have to experiment with all of these categories on your own, to see what Painter 2016 offers. One of the most useful brushes for production work that we've not yet covered yet is the **PatternPen**. The reason this is powerful is that it uses seamless patterns. This lets you draw tiling art.

The Pattern Pen: Painting with Seamless Patterns

Start by launching Corel Painter 2016 and use a **File ➤ New** menu sequence to create a NetBook (1024x600) resolution blank Canvas layer. Name your file `Digital_Painting_Techniques_CH14_PatternPen.rif`, and select the **Pebble Boards Paper** and set the **Pink** color using the Color Palette. Next, use a **Windows ➤ Media Library Panels ➤ Patterns** menu sequence to open the **Pattern Libraries** palette, shown circled in red in Figure 14-1, and Select the **PatternPen** Brush category and **Pattern Pen** brush variant, shown selected in green. Notice that since your brush paints with a pattern, that the brush color is not used, only the colors from your pattern.

Figure 14-1. *Select the PatternPen and open the Pattern palette*

Select the seamless pattern you want to paint with, then paint onto the blank canvas. This takes some getting used to for seamless connecting patterns, so draw a large circle on the canvas, and try to make the pattern connect seamlessly near the top of the circle. It's not easy, at least not until you get used to this brush, which as you will see is very powerful.

I wanted to show some of the more useful tiling pattern brush strokes in Painter, which are shown as in Figure 14-2, so I chose a zipper, rope (or steel cable), and link chain pattern, so that you can see the professional result you can achieve for your artwork by painting with a seamless pattern.

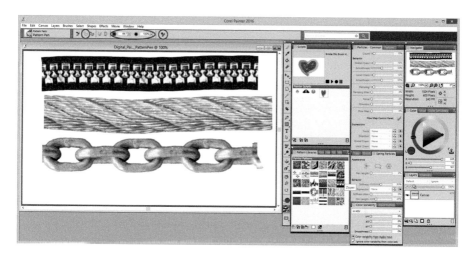

Figure 14-2. *Draw out Zipper, Rope, and Chain seamless patterns*

I covered how to create seamless patterns using GIMP 2.8 in Chapter 4 of this book as well as in my *Digital Illustration Fundamentals* (Apress, 2015) book. I also have fundamentals books covering digital audio, digital video, and digital imaging.

As you can see at the top of Figure 14-2, the PatternPen uses the primary or main brush characteristics that are always available in your icon bar, next to the drop-down Painter Brush selector. I selected the **freehand** (curves) line type and a **66.7** brush size, and a **100%** brush opacity (transparency) as are seen circled in red along with an icon on the far right, which opens up the **Advanced Brush Controls** palettes. Let's click that next.

When you click on the **Advanced Brush Controls icon**, seen in blue in Figure 14-3, the Advanced Brush Control palettes are opened up, as shown on the right side of the Painter toolbar.

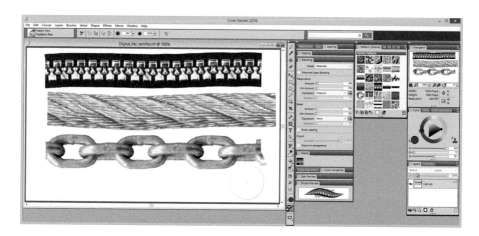

Figure 14-3. *Open Advanced Brush Controls palette with the Dot-Brush icon (top left)*

You can also see the ghost brush outline, in the bottom right of the screenshot. To open and close palette panel tabs, double-click on the tab itself, to open and close that panel. I opened the Size, Opacity, and Stroke Preview tabs since they are the ones we're using, and I selected an Impasto brush category, as can be seen in Figure 14-4.

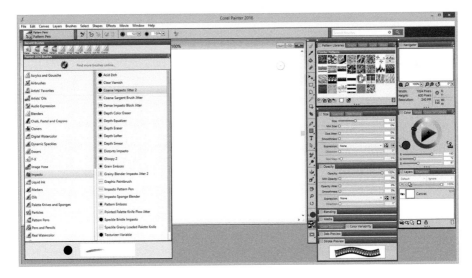

Figure 14-4. *Open Size and Opacity Tabs; select Impasto Brushes*

Impasto brushes look like very thick oil paint, like oil paint that is applied using a spackling knife, and look very 3D as you will soon see, especially when you paint over a previous brush stroke. I chose a **Coarse Impasto Jitter 2** brush variant, which has a complex brush tip, as you will see in Figure 14-5.

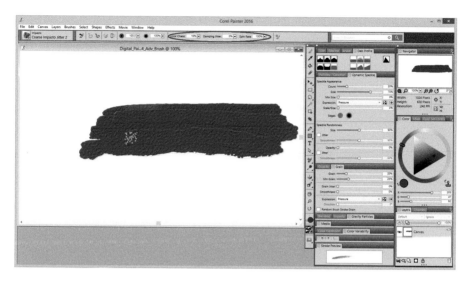

Figure 14-5. *Advanced Brush palette changes to support Impasto*

It is interesting to notice that Painter will change the configuration of both the brush toolbar at the top of Painter, as well as the Advanced Brush Controls palette, as can be seen in Figure 14-5. Painter will automatically add controls to the toolbar, as shown circled in red, and open and close your tabs in the Advanced Brush Controls palette, showing you where you should adjust brush parameters to control this brush variant.

I picked a cinnamon color by using the color wheel outer Hue selector to pick a Red hue and then dragged the plus icon internal to the inner triangle to dull the color a bit, making it more realistic.

I painted the strokes using the Jitter algorithm, which has a brush tip much like the Spring Particles brush we looked at earlier in the book, as you see on the left in Figure 14-5.

You can see the 3D texture in the paint, as well as a 3D build-up in the strokes that are on top of previous strokes in Figure 14-5 if you look very carefully. This shows that Painter can be used to simulate real-world natural media digital paint.

In the digital painting programming environment we cover in the book, you can see how advanced the algorithms, workflows and techniques are for the digital painting software genre. The advanced digital painting topics continue in remaining chapters covering programming and publishing, which show you how you can code and deliver multi-layer (composite) digital paintings, and even make them interactive on today's popular hardware devices.

The Eraser Brush: Bleach Colors, Leaving Texture

We've already looked at Painter's **Eraser Tool**, back in Chapter 7 (reference Figure 7-4), which erases all pixels on the active layer or even on the Canvas layer, which I call the "backplate" or background layer for a digital painting composition. You may be wondering if there is a more advanced and flexible way to erase or modify pixels in a more painterly fashion, and indeed you can, using the Painter **Erasers Brush** collection. One of the more interesting brush variants in this collection allows you to bleach color out of a digital painting while retaining contrast and luminosity (lights and shadows) values. Since this would be appropriate to show using the Impasto 3D Oil Paint brush variants we have been looking at, let's do this next. Drop down the Painter Brushes selector, as seen in Figure 14-6, and select the Erasers Brush category, and the **Pointed Bleach** brush variant, so we can drip bleach using surgical accuracy.

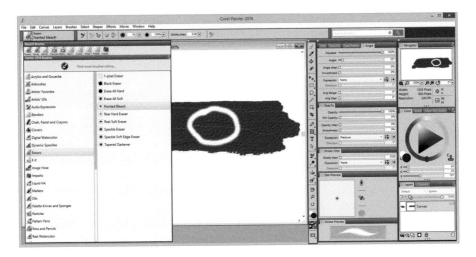

Figure 14-6. *Use a Pointed Bleach Eraser brush and bleach paint*

I combined a circular Pointed Bleach Eraser Brush stroke with your drop-down menu, so as to use only one screen shot for this section of the chapter. As you can see, the color is gone, but the texture of the Impasto Paint Brush variant remains. The Eraser Brush variants can therefore provide artists with a much more powerful and versatile way of erasing than the Eraser Tool can provide, by allowing all of the brush characteristics to be put into play in your paint strokes erasing work process. Next, let's take a look at a similar brush category that uses colors already on the canvas to blend into your **Blender** brush strokes.

The Blenders Brush: Affecting Colors on a Canvas

Another advanced brush similar to an Eraser Brush type that is very similar is the Blender Brush type. Like the Erasers Brush variants, the Blenders Brush variants affect the pixels (color) that has already been painted on the Canvas. The primary difference is that the underlying pixels are modified rather than being erased. For instance, there is a liquid water, smear, blur, glazing effect, and similar blending effects, which use the underlying pixels on the Canvas as the source for the brush stroke dynamics engine. To see this blending effect better, use the 3D rendered car PNG24 image from your book repository and select the Blenders Brush category and the Particle Spring Soft Blender 2 brush variant, as can be seen in Figure 14-7. Notice the **Glow** option for dark color use, and **Stiffness** value for the Spring physics. Also, Advanced Brush Controls are off (closed).

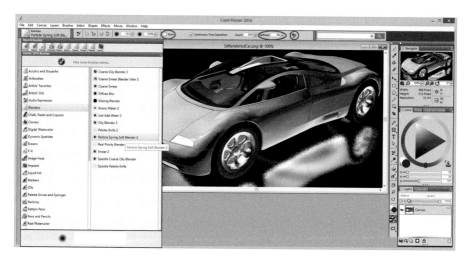

Figure 14-7. *Open 3dRenderedCar.png and select Blenders brushes*

Click the Advanced Brush Control icon and open the brush control tabs, seen on the left in Figure 14-8. Set **Stiffness** to 18% and **Color Variability** to Hue 16%, Saturation 20%, Value 25%, and Smoothness 25%. Set the Spacing **Boost** to 10%, **Grain** to 20%, **Particle Weight** to 25%, and **Weight Jitter** to 10%, as is seen in Figure 14-8. I also tried enabling the **Glow** option but it added too much White coloration to the brushstroke, so I disabled it.

Figure 14-8. *Try Glow, set 18% Stiffness, set army green color*

Now, double-click the brush control tabs that you've set parameters in to close them, and double-click your **Blending** and **Color Expression** tabs to open them to set even more parameters.

I maxed the **Resaturation** value to **100%** and set a **Minimum** Resaturation to **50%** and based the Resaturation on the **Direction** of the Brushstroke, for those of you who are using your mouse.

I set the **Bleed** value to **60%**, and set a **Minimum** Bleed of **30%**. I algorithmically based the Bleed value on the **Velocity** of the Brushstroke, again for those readers who are using a mouse.

I selected the **Dryout to Transparency** option as I wanted some of the car image to show through my brushstrokes, and then I set the **Color Expression** tab parameters. I set a **Color Jitter** parameter to **75%**, and the **Smoothness** to **100%**. I algorithmically based Color Expression values on Brushstroke **Velocity** for those readers using a mouse. Now it is time to test these settings.

As you can see, at the end of the brush stroke in Figure 14-9, you can actually see your Spring Particle Brush Tips, and you can see the color variation and opacity blending with the car image background pixel values. As you can see, Painter will be useful for applying special effects to digital photographs, once you master hundreds of advanced brush control parameters.

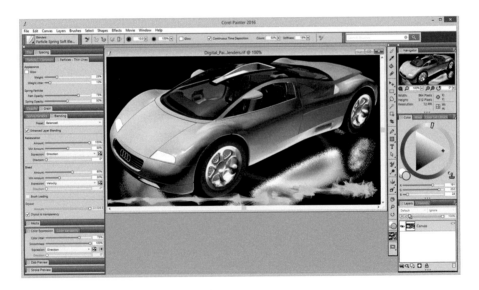

Figure 14-9. *Set Blending and Color Expression, and test brush*

Next, let's take a look at yet another group of brushes, called Painter **F-X** brush variants. These apply **special effects**, to photographic, or painterly, pixels in your Canvas backplate.

The F-X Brushes: Brushing In Special Effects

There's another group of Painter 2016 brush variants that, like the Erasers and Blenders, also affect the Canvas (pixel color). These are called **F-X Brushes**, which is short for **Effects**, which is, in turn, short for **Special Effects**. These include things such as applying distortion, fog, glow, bubbles, marbling, hurricane effects, and even color gradients. Select the F-X brush group and the Marbling Rake brush variant, as shown on the left in Figure 14-10, and stroke the brush across your current image. I also Marble-Rake the previous brush effect, showing how you can use more than one paintbrush in a series to achieve the result.

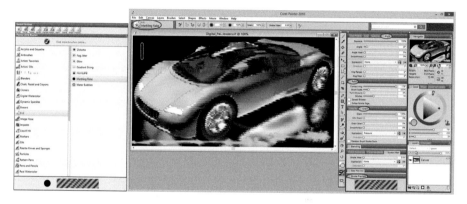

Figure 14-10. *Select Marbling Rake F-X brush variant and use it*

As you'll see in Figure 14-11, Painter has automatically reconfigured the Advanced Brush Tools floating palette with tab headings for the major settings for this tool, including **Angle**, **Rake**, **Grain**, **Blending** and **Stroke Preview**, shown circled in red. As you can see, **Grain** is set at 100%, as is **Angle Squeeze**. Your **Rake** settings are the most important, with a **178** degree **Contact Angle**, **330% Brush Scale** and **10 Bristles**.

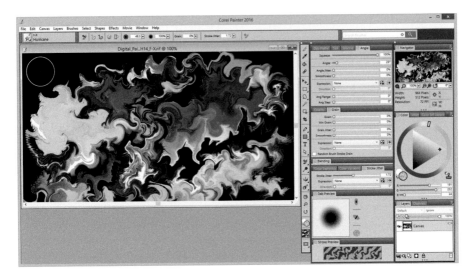

Figure 14-11. *Select the Hurricane F-X brush variant and use it*

One of the great learning tools in Painter 2016 is this feature, which allows you to study the settings for these Brush Variants to see how these effects are created, and then "tweak" these settings gradually, to really examine how they affect the digital paint brushing work process.

This will of course be unique for each artist, therefore there is no way around the time (experience) that you will need to spend with this advanced digital painting software to become one with it. As said universally: "May the Brush be with you!"

Let's apply another one of the effects that is far more extreme, the **Hurricane F-X Brush**. As you can see in Figure 14-11, this effect is even more distorted, but it's fun to apply!

As you can see, this brush setting has 0% Grain and high Stroke Jitter of 1.72 (172%). As you can see in the Dab Preview tab, this brush has a blur edge, which serves to anti-alias, or smooth, the Hurricane brush stroke edges. You can see an effect for these brush settings in the Stroke Preview tab in real time as you adjust brush parameters in all of these different tabs.

Next let's take a look at a Fog Jitter F-X brush variant, which happens to be fantastic for creating background imagery, or even graphics that can be used for seamless tiling imagery for the Web, pattern fills, texture maps, or for applications.

Save and close your car image, and use a **File ➤ New** menu sequence, and open the **New Image** dialog, shown in Figure 14-12. Name the project `Digital_Painting_Techniques_CH14_FogJitter.rif`, and a NetBook **1024x600** resolution. Use a **White** default color and the **Intricate Tracing** paper preset.

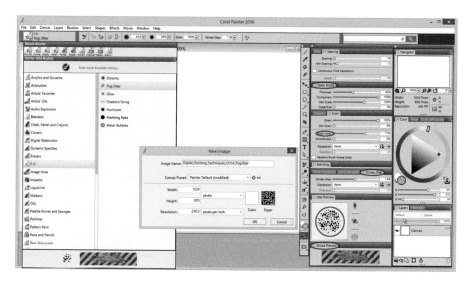

Figure 14-12. *Create a New Image, and select a Fog Jitter brush*

Select your **Fog Jitter** brush variant from your **F-X** Brush collection, and notice that the Advanced Brush Controls palette tabs changed drastically, bringing up **Static Bristle**, **Blending**, **Grain**, **Spacing**, and the Dab Preview and Stroke Preview tabs.

Especially interesting is the Dab Preview tab, which has a brush "Dab" profile image in it that looks pretty cool. This is called a "Dab," because this is what the brush stroke should look like if you simply "dabbed" a brush on the Canvas (clicked the mouse once for instance). This is what makes the Fog Jitter brush work so well for painting background pattern imagery.

As you can see in Figure 14-13, I have not changed Army Green as my base color or my color variation parameters, thus, I am getting that same "camouflage" type of color spectrum. The **Grain Jitter** of 71% and **Stroke Jitter** of 1.94 give the brush a nice randomized effect, in conjunction with the **Static Bristle** settings of 720% Hair Scale and 43% Static Bristle Thickness.

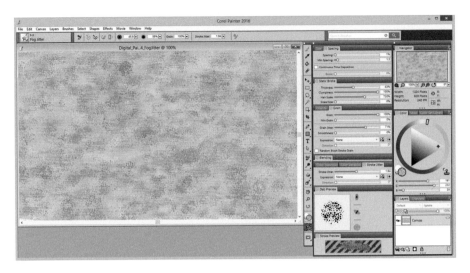

Figure 14-13. *Create a background texture, using F-X Fog Jitter*

Smart Strokes: Traditional Brushes Using Effects

Next, let's take a look at a traditional Acrylics Brush variant that incorporates pattern data; I'll use the Zipper pattern, in the brushing algorithm. This type of brush can be found in your **Smart Strokes** brush category or grouping. Create a new project, and select the Smart Strokes **Acrylics Dry Brush**, as is shown in Figure 14-14. Select a Pattern from a Pattern floating palette, or a Pattern floating toolbar, or your Pattern Library floating palette, and then paint using the Acrylic Dry Brush variant. As you can see the Smart Strokes category adds special effects, in this case it's subtle pattern data in the brush stroke and can provide some really impressive digital painting special effects into your already impressive digital paint compositing arsenal.

As you can see in Figure 14-14, the primary parameter for this brush is the Bristles Feature setting of 3.9 and a pattern with an Opacity setting of 25% and a slight 0.04 Stroke Jitter.

184

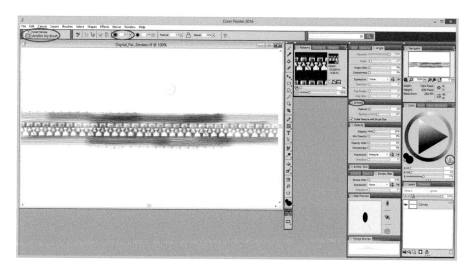

Figure 14-14. *Using the Smart Strokes Acrylic Dry Brush pattern*

As you can see, the Color Wheel Picker is currently in a grayscale mode, giving us a nice pencil sketch effect, shown in Figure 14-14 on the Canvas, as I brushed a few strokes to test.

Next, let's take a look at how you would introduce color to the brush variant, creating your own Acrylic Dry Color Brush variant. First, set your Color Picker Sliders, at the bottom of the Color palette. I used the setting of Green 126 and Blue 167 to give me a nice Teal color. Next I clicked on the **Clone Color** icon, which is shown circled in red, in Figure 14-15.

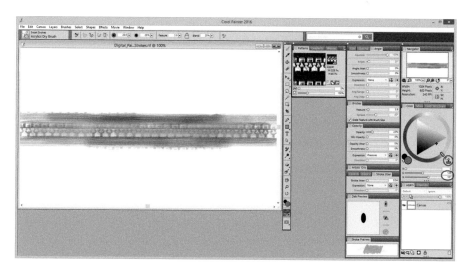

Figure 14-15. *Set a Teal color, and click the Clone Color Icon*

Once you click the Clone Color Icon the Color Wheel will become colored again and you can select colors. After testing a Teal color, as shown in Figure 14-15, I dialed in a Pink color, and tested that in Figure 14-16. Also notice that once color is enabled, the Stroke Preview will show how color factors in the stroke dynamics result. Compare this Stroke Preview change, from Figure 14-14 to both Figure 14-15 as well as Figure 14-16.

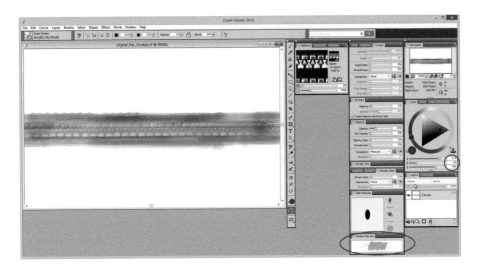

Figure 14-16. *Select a Pink color and notice the Stroke Preview*

I could continue going through Painter Brush categories and analyzing brush variant parameters for another 10 thousand pages, however, there are a lot of other advanced concepts that I need to cover regarding "bridging" your digital painting art over to modern consumer electronics devices, operating systems, content publishing platforms, and programming languages. I will do this during the final two chapters of this book, so that you will have a comprehensive overview regarding how this technical information that you learned during the book extends beyond the content production software tools, to popular operating systems or publishing platforms. Leveraging these more advanced content delivery systems allows you to add gamification, interactivity, and edutainment into your digital painting artwork, and content assets. This will give you the order of magnitude more artistic power as a digital painter that you're seeking to differentiate yourself and your content creation pipeline.

Summary

In this fourteenth chapter, we looked at Corel Painter 2016 brush variants to see what goes into the design of the brush presets as well as your own custom brush variants in the future as you continue to master Corel Painter 2016. As you have probably realized by now, the Corel Brush Packs that offer additional brush variants to Corel Painter 2016 are actually just collections of settings for Painter 2016's brushing engine that create all new digital paint brush variants simply by using new settings for the nearly infinite combination of parameters that are possible using the Painter Brushing Engine.

We looked at several more of Painter's brush categories, including the PatternPen, F-X Brushes, Smart Strokes, Blenders, Erasers, Acrylic and Impasto, as well as more Particle Brushes.

We looked at how you can analyze current brush variants, to see how they produce the digital painting results that they create. We looked at how to tweak different parameters so that you can better understand, through experimentation and through experience, how the Painter 2016 digital paintbrush algorithms will process these settings, turning them into amazing, useful digital painting tools. The more time you spend with Painter, the more amazing the digital painting results you will produce.

In Chapter 15, we will take a look at incorporating your digital painting into your interactive programming workflow, or using Painter 2016 **scripting,** in case you haven't added Java or HTML5 programming into your toolset yet. After that we will get into consumer electronics device publishing topics to finish up the book.

■ ■ ■

CHAPTER 15

The Automation of Digital Painting: Programming

Now that you have learned how to create professional digital painting content pipelines using powerful brushes, algorithms, and digital image compositing features in digital illustration and digital painting software packages such as Inkscape and Painter 2016, let's take a look at how to leverage your SVG and PNG data that these software packages generate (export) using the most popular and widespread vector and raster file formats in a few of the most popular programming platforms. The reason we're taking a look at these open content programming platforms themselves is because I wanted to cover Java and HTML5 just in case you wanted to take your digital painting compositing career to the next level, which would involve interactivity and gamification.

During the chapter you'll learn about delivering digital painting (PNG) and digital illustration (SVG) content using the popular open source programming languages that support digital imagery PNG and digital illustration SVG formats. These include Java 8, JavaFX 8, HTML5, CSS3, JavaScript, and XML, for content development using Android Studio, iOS, Blackberry OS, Tizen OS, Mozilla Firefox OS, Opera OS, Google Chrome OS, and Windows OS.

This is important information if you plan to use digital painting or digital illustration you've created for programming projects using **open software development platforms**. If you have an interest in learning more about adding programming into your vast digital content production and publishing repertoire, this chapter will give you the head start in beginning that journey.

Content Delivery Programming Platforms

Several platforms run the majority of the Consumer Electronics Industry hardware devices. They include **Java** (Android Studio or WebKit), **JavaFX** (Android, iOS, Windows, Linux, Mac OS X, Solaris), and **JavaScript** with CSS3 and HTML5 scripting (WebKit Browsers).

This chapter is not going to teach you programming, for that would take an number of books (and coding experience), but it will expose you to what's possible if you extend the journey you're on from digital painting and digital illustration to new media software development. Everything that we will be covering in the chapter is free for commercial use! You can download XML and HTML5 (NetBeans 8.1), Android Studio (IntelliJ), Java 8 and JavaFX, and JavaScript, which are all included with NetBeans 8.1.

Before we get into the Painter scripting language, let's start off with what I'll call "external" programming languages. The most widespread application development language is Java 8, including its JavaFX New Media Engine API. These can be used to develop applications for Android Studio, Windows, Linux, Mac OS X, iOS, and Solaris operating systems, as well as web sites, or IoT.

Java 7, 8, 9 and JavaFX: The javafx.scene.effect API

Digital painting and digital illustration compositing pipelines can be built and controlled using code in the Java programming language, as can be seen in Figure 15-1. The backplate imagery is a PNG24, the 3D logo is a PNG32, and the script text images are PNG32 as well. The text is vector artwork and could contain SVG objects created in Inkscape as well using the same code. Java has a library called **JavaFX** that provides expansive new media asset support spanning digital illustration (SVG) and digital painting (PNG), as well as digital imaging, digital audio, digital video, and i3D real-time OpenGL rendering. Most of the digital illustration data, filters, and XML we have been using during this book are in the **javafx.scene.shape** library and the **javafx.scene.effects** library. JavaFX 8 applications run in HTML5, Linux, Windows, Solaris, Mac, Android, or iOS; thus Java, the world's most popular programming language, is truly "code once, deliver everywhere."

Figure 15-1. *Compositing raster and vector assets using JavaFX8*

The splash screen for a game I am coding, for my upcoming *Pro Java Games Development* title (Apress, 2016), can be seen in Figure 15-1. The upper-left quadrant is the splash screen itself and uses a PNG24 backplate image overlaid with PNG32 composite images (two), vector (text) elements, and user interface button elements. Since digital painting assets should be PNG24 you can simply substitute your digital painting assets for the rendered 3D assets shown as the background imagery here for your digital illustration and digital painting workflow, using the same file formats that I use here, and the exact same Java 8 and JavaFX 8 programing logic, unless Java 9 has come out (in October 2016).

As you can see, the quality level afforded by Java 8 and JavaFX 8 is amazing, and available for playback on nearly every popular platform, including Android, iOS, Blackberry, Firefox, Opera, Chrome, Windows, Linux, Solaris, and Mac OS X.

The Java and JavaFX code can be seen in Figure 15-2. The JavaFX API is contained in the Java API; thus, JavaFX is Java.

Figure 15-2. JavaFX code adds raster and vector assets to games

These were originally two separate programming languages until JavaFX was acquired by Sun Microsystems, right before Sun was acquired by Oracle.

I show the code for two of the buttons, the **Instructions** button and the **Copyrights** button, which I called **helpButton** and **legalButton** in my Java code, seen in Figure 15-2. I do not seek to teach you Java programming during this chapter; however, Java syntax is understandable enough to explain to you what is going on for this media compositing pipeline example, so, here we go!

The boardGameBackPlate.setImage(transparentLogo) Java statement is changing my digital image asset in my **backplate layer**, using terms that you are now familiar with from this book.

The colorAdjust.setHue(0.4); Java statement **color shifts** the logo 40%, around the color wheel, and the colorAdjust.setHue(-0.4); Java code also color shifts the logo 40% around the color wheel only in the opposite direction. With a color slider it would be 40% to the right and 40% to the left, respectively.

Vertical, Y axis pixel positioning is being accomplished using the infoOverlay. setTranslateY(350); Java code and text spacing is being accomplished using an infoOverlay.setLineSpacing(-12); Java statement. This is how an image compositing pipeline is created using Java code.

As you can see, your digital painting assets and digital illustration assets can be taken to the next level, which would include interactivity, and gamification, using Java and JavaFX programming logic. This is why I am exposing you to this during this chapter, so you know it is there, if you wanted to use it.

Next, let's take a look at layer compositing pipelines, implemented using only basic markup languages (HTML5 and CSS3).

HTML5 and CSS3: Digital Painting Compositing

Whereas Java (JavaFX) is the most popular programming language, HTML5 and CSS3 markup languages are the most widespread as far as usage is concerned. This is because they are used in every browser, which all use an API called **WebKit**, as does Android and iOS, so they are used in these OSes as well. There are also several HTML5 OSes out now, not surprisingly, from the makers of the HTML5 browsers. These include Chrome OS, Firefox OS, and Opera OS. These are used in Smartphones, Tablets, and iTV Sets. Panasonic iTV Sets use Firefox OS, Sony uses Opera OS, Google has a range of Chrome OS products, and Alcatel-Lucent uses Firefox OS.

I composited the HDTV resolution www.iTVset.com web site, using only lossless codecs and with a combination of **PNG24**, **SVG,** and **aniGIF** for backplate sections, as well as **PNG32** for all i3D UI element overlays. As you can see in Figure 15-3, the web site looks like uncompressed truecolor imagery. It is animated using JavaScript, and it's interactive. The site was coded in only 24 lines of HTML5, and less than 2MB for total graphic image asset data footprint. This is made possible by a digital compositing (layer) pipeline, allowing the "granularization" of the digital assets. This allows me to use smaller, faster asset file sizes.

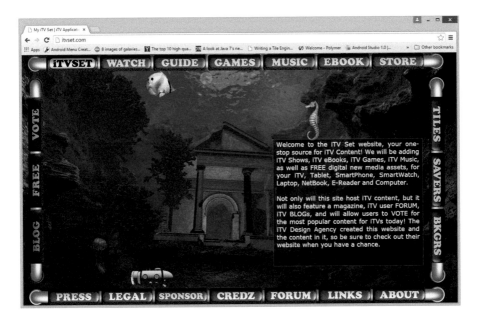

Figure 15-3. *Image Composite Layers using HTML5 and CSS3 markup*

Additionally, a lot of **indexed color** assets can be used, allowing a site that looks like it is truecolor, but in fact is not. For instance, all six animated elements on the page use an indexed color **animGIF** file format with the 1-bit pre-multiplied alpha channel (uses average background color to hide aliasing).

The i3D user interface button elements use **PNG32** format, using its **alpha channel** to composite the UI seamlessly over any background image used in any section of this web site, including digital video, Java (JavaFX) applications, 3D animation as seen on the www.iTVSet.com home page, or full screen imagery.

Graphics elements are held in HTML5 **<DIV>** tags, and CSS3 is used for **blending, opacity**, **positioning** and **interactivity**. I do not obstruct the right-click action with my code in any way, so you can right-click on the site and "View as Source" to look at any of this code, at any time during the site's development.

Text is rendered by WebKit in its own <DIV> tag regions, using HTML5 to define content and metatags and styled with CSS3.

As you can see, just like Java and JavaFX, HTML5 and CSS can provide you with a layer compositing pipeline, which can be almost as powerful as GIMP and Photoshop. However you will have to be a creative and a savvy programmer, in order to pull these capabilities out of open source languages and technologies such as SVG, XML, HTML5, CSS3, and JavaScript, which support all the things we have covered in this book, such as SVG Filters, Blend Modes, Opacity, Alpha Channels, Layers, Patterns and Gradients.

Android Studio: Java's PorterDuff Blending Modes

Google's Android platform is on more Smartphone, eBook eReader, Tablet, iTV Set, Game Console, Smartwatch, and other IoT device hardware than any other OS platform internationally. If you are interested in developing interactive digital painting content for Android, I wrote a series of **Pro Android** titles for Apress spanning 2013 through 2016. These include *Pro Android Graphics* (2013), *Pro Android UI* (2014), *Pro Android Wearables* (2015), and I am currently writing *Pro Android IoT* (2016). These cover how to use Java code to implement **PorterDuff** pixel blending and pixel transfer modes in the *Pro Android Graphics* title, just like we have used in this book. In fact, Figure 15-4 shows one of the many screenshots from this book, showing three different Android blending modes displayed on the Nexus One AVD Emulator.

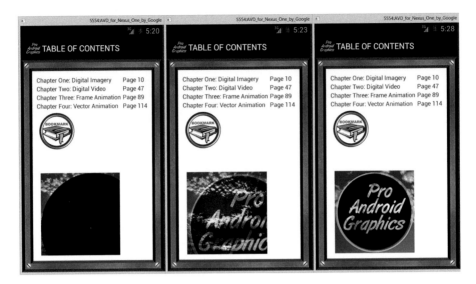

Figure 15-4. *Android's PorterDuff class provides blending modes*

The Java code to put together this compositing pipeline, which has a PNG24 backplate, PNG32 ring element, PNG32 3D logo, and alpha-controlled vector circle, with a black fill color, is fairly complex, as can be seen in Figure 15-5.

Figure 15-5. *Java code for implementing a compositing pipeline*

I will go through what the Java statements do so you can see a Java-based compositing code pipeline that matches up with layer-based compositing pipelines that you have become familiar with during the book in Corel Painter 2016. Android has layers!

Layers are called **LayerDrawable** in Android, so the first line of code loads the LayerDrawable with a **contents_layers.png** asset, by using a getResources(). getDrawable() method call "chain."

I commented out a backgroundImage plate, for testing, so I will just cover the foregroundImage plate code here. I create a Bitmap object named **foregroundImage** and load it with an asset named **cloudsky.png** with a **BitmapFactory.decodeResource()** method call. I make that Bitmap object **mutable** (changeable) by putting it into memory using a **.copy()** method call, specifying an **8-bit ARGB** color depth (this is equivalent to a 32-bit color space).

I then set a PorterDuff **transfer mode** (sometimes called a **blending mode**, although technically some blending modes will transfer pixels rather than blending them together) on a **Paint** object by using the **.setXfermode()** method, using the **XOR** mode.

I create a Drawable object, named **layerOne**, and load it, with a Bitmap object named **composite** and load that into memory as a **mutableComposite**; and using that, I create a Bitmap object named **compositeImage**. I then create a **Canvas** object to draw on named **imageCanvas** and load that with the compositeImage object.

Next, I draw a Bitmap object on the Canvas object, using an **imageCanvas. drawBitmap()** method call. This specifies an area using a square 1,000 pixel **Rect** object, a blending mode using a **paintObject**, and a **mutableForegroundImage** Bitmap object (bitmap or raster imagery that I have specified as 32-bit, ARGB_8888).

I create the **ImageView** named **porterDuffImageComposite** to hold (display) this pipeline in my user interface design, and I load this ImageView by using the **.setImageBitmap()** method call.

Next let's take a look at how Java and JavaFX bridge the two different technologies, raster and vector, together just as Inkscape and Painter 2016 do in their software packages code. I will show you how I created this vector "collision cage," using GIMP, how the SVG Command Data was optimized, and how this data is encapsulated, using the JavaFX SVGPath class.

Game Design: SVG for Collision Detection

As you see in Figure 15-6, I use the **Pen Path Tool** in GIMP to create a collision cage for the InvinciBagel character sprite. One of the run cycle cels is seen here, with only 15 data points to process for the collision polygon. GIMP can save its pen path data using the **SVG XML** format, which allows you to cull the SVG data for use in your programming projects. In this case I used an SVG path to create a **collision polygon** cage for a game sprite.

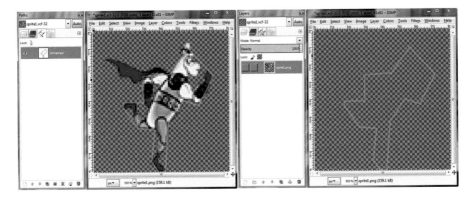

Figure 15-6. SVG data used for a game sprite collision polygon

Figure 15-7 shows **raw SVG XML data**, exported using GIMP, using the **SVG XML** format, prior to data footprint optimization.

```
spritelsvghand - Notepad
File  Edit  Format  View  Help
<?xml version="1.0" encoding="UTF-8" standalone="no"?>
<!DOCTYPE svg PUBLIC "-//W3C//DTD SVG 20010904//EN"
"http://www.w3.org/TR/2001/REC-SVG-20010904/DTD/svg10.dtd">
<svg xmlns="http://www.w3.org/2000/svg" width="1.125in" height="1.125in" viewBox="0 0 81 81">
   <path id="Unnamed" fill="none" stroke="black" stroke-width="1"
         d="M 56.73,10.00
            C 56.73,10.00 45.82,25.09 45.82,25.09
              45.82,25.09 30.18,26.36 30.18,26.36
              30.18,26.36 30.00,40.55 30.00,40.55
              30.00,40.55 18.00,40.73 18.00,40.73
              18.00,40.73 17.82,44.36 17.82,44.36
              17.82,44.36 26.91,56.00 26.91,56.00
              26.91,56.00 37.45,56.73 37.45,56.73
              37.45,56.73 34.91,74.91 34.91,74.91
              34.91,74.91 38.55,80.91 38.55,80.91
              38.55,80.91 42.73,80.73 42.73,80.73
              42.73,80.73 44.91,52.91 44.91,52.91
              44.91,52.91 53.82,40.18 53.82,40.18
              53.82,40.18 62.91,42.55 62.91,42.55
              62.91,42.55 72.36,26.36 72.36,26.36 ▨" /> </svg>
```

Figure 15-7. SVG XML data from Pen Tool path exported from GIMP

As you will see in Figure 15-8, I reduced the coordinate pairs from 45 to 15, yielding a **300%** data footprint reduction. These vertex data coordinate X,Y pairs are what we would use in an SVGPath class (object) in Java or JavaFX to render the data.

Figure 15-8. *Optimize SVG Command String data; select for Java*

I copied the data into an **Array** object in Java as a subobject called **spriteFrame** in my **iBagel** object. So, to reference the data, I use iBagel.spriteFrame, and to access the **invinciBagel** class, an even larger object, I use invinciBagel.iBagel.spriteFrame, as can be seen in green, on Java code line **122**, in Figure 15-9.

Figure 15-9. *Collision detection Java code referencing SVG data*

To turn this collision polygon data into something that JavaFX can use, I call the .getBoundsInParent().intersects() method, creating a Shape intersection object that determines collision.

Your first intersection of collision polygons determines collisions, that is, the objects have barely touched each other and your program logic would then determine what happens in the game based on these object (collision polygon) collisions.

You can see the JavaFX code in Figure 15-9 executing for the game in Figure 15-10. As you can see, Java and JavaFX allow you to create some impressive multimedia productions using your digital imaging, digital painting, or digital illustration data. This data is "bridged over" from your content production tools, using PNG8, PNG24, and PNG32 as well as SVG command formats, and even digital audio and video data, using MPEG-4 data formats.

Figure 15-10. *JavaFX combines raster imagery with vector assets*

As you can see, all of the concepts that we have covered during the course of this book are available in Java and JavaFX using the powerful JavaFX Pulse Engine and its new media APIs.

You can also bet that all these concepts have support in each of the major open content distribution platforms including Android, iOS, Java, JavaFX, HTML5, CSS3, JavaScript, and Kindle.

The reason for this is because these platforms are "open source." Interestingly, so are the data technologies themselves including the PorterDuff modes, OpenGL, JPG, SVG, GIF, PNG, 3D, XML, i3D, alpha channels, PDF, EPS, and even GIMP and Inkscape.

Since all of the areas of digital asset compositing will be "free for commercial use," it is logical for the open source platforms to completely incorporate them. All this is excellent news for digital painting and image compositing aficionados!

Painter 2016 Scripting: Coding for Painter

Next, let's take a look at a programming language inside Corel Painter. Actually Painter has a "scripting" language, which is **higher-level** than a programming language, and therefore, easier to use. In fact, it is more like a recorder, and allows you to record and save actions in

Painter in a "script." These actions can be anything from a single "move" as I like to call it, such as applying a menu sequence, to recording an entire compositing session or an entire digital painting artwork creation process. As you can see in Figure 15-11, you'll use the **Window ➤ Scripts** menu sequence in order to open the Scripting floating palettes.

Figure 15-11. *Use Window ➤ Scripts menu sequence; open palettes*

There are **Stop**, **Play**, **Record**, and **Pause** transport icons, in the **Scripts** palette, you can use to control your scripting, or you can use the **Utility Icon** in the top-right of the palette to access menu items for these features, as well as all of your other scripting features. These are shown circled in red, along with the brush and tool you are going to use, to record some of your paint strokes to see how this scripting function operates.

Let's record some paint strokes and see how this feature works. Press the **Record** button or select **Record Script** from the Utility Icon menu, and paint the right side of a heart using an orange color as is shown in the Color wheel selector palette on the far-right side of Figure 15-11. I used a Bristle Oils brush shown circled in red in Figure 15-11 along with the brush tool.

I changed my Color to an orange-red color and painted in the other side of the heart. Next, I used a red and pink color, and painted inside of this heart. I did all this painting while the record button (function) was active in the Script palette.

When I was finished painting these five brush strokes, I hit the **Stop** button and was presented with a **Script Name** dialog that I used to name the script **Bristle Oils Brush Heart**, as you can see at the bottom of Figure 15-12.

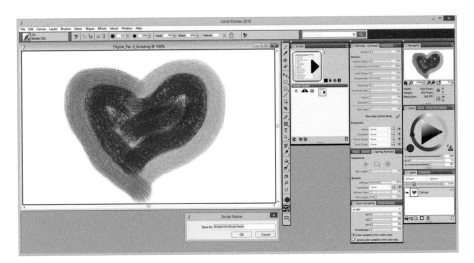

Figure 15-12. *Record Painting a Heart, and assign a Script Name*

After I hit the **OK** button, the finished script showed up in the main **Scripts** palette, as well as in the **Painter Scripts** icon selector area located underneath the Scripts palette. This can be seen in Figure 15-13 along with an **Export Script** dialog.

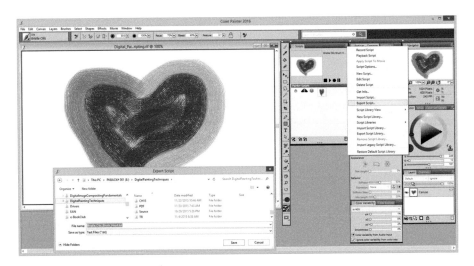

Figure 15-13. *Use the Export Script dialog and save script text*

The reason I am showing you the import and export script features, is because there is a robust "third party scripting" marketplace, where Painter users can trade their scripts, so if you want to show off your painting skills or compositing moves, this is the basic script recording and exporting workflow which you will utilize to accomplish this.

One such script trader forum is on the www.WetCanvas.com website. The script trading forum located at the following URL:

http://www.wetcanvas.com/forums/archive/index.php/t-308210.html.

As you can see on the menu for the **Scripts Utility Icon**, you can also delete scripts, edit script text, Get Info on the script, manage Script Libraries, and set your Painter Scripting Options. The Script Options dialog can be seen in Figure 15-14, and allows you to **Save Frames on Playback**, **Record Initial State** and set the script **recording time** (sampling) value using tenths of a second accuracy.

Figure 15-14. *Painter 2016 Script Options dialog*

If you wanted to travel into Painter's fourth dimension, make sure to master the scripting, digital video and animation features in Painter 2016, as I was not able to cover all of the features of Painter 2016 (there are thousands) in this one book title.

Summary

In the Fifteenth chapter, we looked at advanced topics relating to scripting and programming, and how different open languages support your digital asset compositing pipelines, either inside digital media compositing software as your work process, or SVG special effects plug-ins, or SVG XML markup, or outside your digital media compositing software, for taking your creations to a new level by adding interactivity or other useful features such as gamification which are limited only by the imagination.

First you looked at several popular open source platform programming languages and how these could be utilized to create the same digital asset compositing effects which you can create using Inkscape, GIMP, or Painter 2016, all of which are covered in this book. Next, you looked at Java and its JavaFX new media engine and how that platform supports digital asset compositing including advanced blending mode and special effect algorithms.

Then you looked at HTML5 and CSS3, and saw this platform could also implement the digital asset compositing concepts and techniques you learned in this book using only markup languages for deliverables such as websites and HTML5 OS applications.

Next, you looked at using SVG Command data in Java games to create collision detector polygons that are highly optimized for using a smaller amount of system memory.

You looked at Java's PorterDuff class, and some advanced Java code that demonstrated that complex compositing pipelines, with advanced blending modes, can be coded in Java 8 and JavaFX or used in a current version of Android Studio for the creation advanced digital image compositing savvy applications.

JavaFX applications also work with iOS, Windows, Linux, Blackberry, Solaris, Android, Tizen and soon other HTML5 OSes.

Finally, we looked at the Painter 2016 Scripting Engine, and learned the basic workflow for recording a digital painting operation, compositing and effects "moves" or an actual digital painting stroke creation from start to finish, so that digital painting creations can be animated from a blank canvas into the reality of the digital universe.

In the next chapter 16, we will take a closer look at some of the most widespread and popular content publishing platforms and the hardware device types that they are hosted on. It is important to consider where your digital painting assets are going to be viewed.

CHAPTER 16

■ ■ ■

Publishing Digital Painting: Content Delivery Platforms

Now that you have some exposure to fundamental concepts, techniques, and principles spanning digital painting, digital illustration, digital image compositing, and scripting, it is time to take a closer look at how digital painting content can be **published** using popular open source publishing platforms. I'm going to delineate this chapter based upon **consumer electronics hardware device genres**. Devices support different types of applications. For instance, **eBook eReaders**, such as Amazon's Kindle Fire, use Kindle KF8 format; **Smartwatches** use Android Wear SDK under the Android Studio 1.4, using the Android OS 5.4 API; **iTV Sets** use the **Android TV** SDK in Android Studio 1.4, using the Android OS 5.4 API; **Automobile Dashboards** use **Android Auto** SDK with the Android Studio 1.4 IDE with the Android OS 5.4 API; **Tablets** and **Smartphones** use Android SDK in Android Studio 1.4 IDE with the Android OS 5.4 API; **Laptops** and **NetBooks** use Java with JavaFX; and each of these hardware devices also support all of the open industry publishing standards, such as PDF, HTML5, and EPUB3.

We'll continue to look at how to publish with electronic hardware device types, using the software development platforms that these devices support, such as Kindle KF8, EPUB3, Android Studio 1.4 (Android OS 5.4), Java 7, Java 8, Java 9, JavaFX 8, PDF, SVG, XML, HTML5, CSS3, and JavaScript.

Open Source Formats: PDF, HTML, EPUB

Let's start with the content publishing formats that support digital painting that have been defined by industry groups, as **EPUB** and **HTML** have, or which have been "open sourced" as the Adobe **Portable Document Format**, or **PDF**, has been. Each of these formats also supports SVG (digital illustration) format, as you will see during this section of the chapter. I am starting with these open formats, as they are usable across every type of hardware device so I'll start with platforms with wide support.

Portable Document Format: Digital Illustration PDF

The Adobe PDF Portable Document format is utilized by the Adobe **Acrobat Reader**, used around the world for publishing rich media documents that can include **digital painting**, digital audio, digital video, digital imagery, or digital illustration. Acrobat Reader is free and its **PDF** format has been open sourced. The **Adobe Acrobat Professional** series of publishing tools are still paid software packages and well worth the money, if you need to publish via this widely accepted rich media document publishing format. This PDF format supports two digital illustration formats, **EPS** and **PostScript**, the best option being EPS, as far as your quality to file size ratio is concerned. This is because the PDF file format will keep the vector data intact and render it at whatever screen size is being used. You can also use Inkscape to export to EPS, PostScript, and even to PDF directly, so you don't need PDF to support SVG directly, which it does not, probably because it is a competing vector format.

It used to be a .PDF was only used for creating business documents. However, it has been adopted for an eBook format; in fact, you might be reading my books using the PDF format. Other eBook formats include Kindle (.MOBI) and EPUB (EPUB3), which we will be covering later on during this chapter as well.

Another advantage of this PDF document publishing format is that it offers **Digital Rights Management** (DRM) support. This allows you to copy protect (lock) your document if you want to sell it for money. Adobe has a PDF Server product incorporating this DRM feature that allows you to better market PDF content.

It is rumored that the other two publishing formats that we are covering in this section of the chapter are also looking at adding DRM support in the future. Let's look at HTML5 next.

Hypertext Markup Language: HTML Digital Painting

You've already taken a look at how to use SVG and PNG formats during this book, and thus, you know HTML5 supports the SVG digital illustration format, as well as the **PNG8, PNG24, PNG32, JPEG, GIF,** and **AnimGIF** digital painting imagery file formats.

It used to be that HTML5 was only used for creating your web site designs, until the web browser manufacturers decided to utilize their web browser code to create **HTML5 OSs** for consumer electronics devices given the success of Android, Bada, and iOS.

Putting this browser code, with **app launch icon** support, on top of the **Linux OS Kernel**, produced a **Chrome OS** (Motorola), **Firefox OS** (Panasonic iTV), and **Opera OS** (Sony Bravia iTV Sets).

There's also **Tizen OS** (Samsung), which is managed by The Linux Foundation for the creator of the Linux OS Linus Torvalds.

Tizen also uses HTML5. HTML5 is easy to implement thanks to your open source **WebKit API**, which is also a part of Android Studio 1.4 (currently at Android OS 5.4 and soon, Android 6.0).

HTML5 application and web site publishing is therefore an excellent way to deliver content across all embedded mobile OS, desktop OS, and web browser platforms. This is why DRM is in the future of HTML5 and is freely available to you for implementing digital painting assets, by using PNG, SVG, HTML5, JS, and CSS3.

Next, let's take a closer look at the open source EPUB 3 publishing standard, used for e-books, and soon for much more.

Electronic Publishing: Digital Painting in EPUB3

The EPUB specification is a distribution and interchange format standard for digital publications and documents. EPUB 3, the third major release of the open EPUB standard, consists of four specifications, each defining an important component of an overall EPUB document. **EPUB Publications 3** defines publication-level semantics, as well as conformance requirements for EPUB 3 documents. **EPUB Content Documents 3** defines XHTML, SVG, and CSS3 profiles for use in the context of your EPUB 3.0 Publications. **EPUB Open Container Format 3.0**, or OCF3, defines a file format, as well as a processing model for encapsulating sets of related resource assets in one single ZIP file format (EPUB Container). **EPUB Media Overlays 3.0** defines a format and a processing model for the data synchronization of text with digital media assets.

EPUB 3.0 has been widely adopted as a format for digital books, also popularly known as "e-books." This 3.0 specification significantly increase the EPUB format's capability, so that it would be capable of supporting a range of new media publication requirements. These would include complex layout, new media and interactivity, and international typography (fonts) support.

The hope is that EPUB 3 should be utilized for a broader range of content, including e-books; magazines; and educational, professional, artistic and scientific publications.

EPUB 3 supports SVG digital illustration embedded in the document using SVG, and digital painting using PNG, JPEG, or GIF formats. They would inherit the same functions and feature sets that these formats will provide your digital painting in HTML5.

Another impressive new media feature in EPUB 3 is called **Media Overlay Documents**. Media Overlay Documents should be used with SVG documents, such as we saved in Inkscape for this book. Media Overlay Documents also provide the ability to synchronize your digital painting creations with vector elements inside the Publishing Content Document (EPUB3 publishing platforms), which could be used for some very powerful presentation capabilities.

Open Platforms: Java, Android, and Kindle

The next set of formats I am going to cover are open source and free for commercial use, but do not run across every hardware device, and are not industry specifications, but instead are owned by major industry hardware and software manufacturers. Oracle owns Java and JavaFX, Google owns Android, and Amazon owns Kindle (.MOBI) and Kindle Fire, which uses the KF8 format. Let's cover these based on the genres or types of consumer electronics devices that these run on, starting with eBook Readers, since the three formats we just covered are all widely used for delivering e-books as well, as you can see on the Apress.com web site, where you purchase your educational titles.

eBook Readers: Kindle Fire, Android, Java or PDF

The eBook Reader hardware device is actually an Android tablet, which is why I added Android into the title for this section of the chapter. The world's most popular eBook Reader, Kindle Fire runs Android OS, as does the Sony eBook Reader, and the Barnes and Noble NOOK eBook Reader. Even Apple iPad runs Kindle, EPUB3, and PDF eBook titles, as do Blackberry tablets and Microsoft Surface tablets. The reason I added Java in the title for this section is that Kindle has Java capabilities for interactive e-books, and Android uses Java as well. Since eBook readers will also read .PDF files, I also added PDF into this title.

Since most eBook Readers are actually Android tablets or iPads, there are a plethora of platforms for delivering digital painting using PNG and SVG for digital illustration content.

This means you will deliver digital illustration content user experiences with Android applications, HTML5 applications, Java applications, HTML5 web sites, Kindle eBooks, EPUB3 eBooks, NOOK eBooks, or interactive new media PDF documents. This gives you a ton of flexibility in publishing digital painting content using PNG formats or digital illustration using SVG using eBook Readers, which are one of the best-selling consumer electronics devices, especially during the holidays, along with iTV Sets.

iTV Sets: Android TV, Java, JavaScript, and HTML5

The **iTV Set**, or interactive television set, is the most recent consumer electronics device to hit the marketplace, and iTV Set devices are expected to explode in sales, during 2015, 2016, and 2017. This is the reason Google has developed a specialized version of Android SDK (Software Development Kit) for iTV Sets, called the **Android TV API** (Application Programming Interface).

There are **HTML5 OS iTV Set** products as well from Samsung (Tizen OS), Panasonic (Firefox OS), and Sony (Opera OS), so the iTV Set consumer electronic device is much like an eBook Reader device, in that it will allow you to create and deliver digital audio content by using **Java** or **JavaFX** (Android, iOS, HTML5 OS), **HTML5** markup, **CSS3,** and **JavaScript** (iOS, Android OS, HTML5 OS).

It's also important to realize that with iTV Set devices, your viewers are going to be paying closer attention to content streams, including digital painting, digital illustration, i3D, digital imagery, digital audio, and digital video.

The viewer paying close attention to your content is not always the case with devices such as Smartphones or automobile dashboards (at least, let's hope not).

If you wanted to deliver your digital painting content across each of these iTV Set device platforms, you should use HTML5. Android and iOS support HTML5, but HTML5 OS and web sites do not support Android and iOS applications. The other side of that decision is that Apple and Google Play have more advanced app stores; therefore if you are going to monetize your digital painting and digital illustration content, you should consider developing apps using Java (Android) or JavaFX (iOS) more than using JavaScript, under HTML5 OSes or HTML5 browsers, although these fully support SVG and PNG for digital painting as well as digital illustration content delivery endeavors.

Smartwatches: Android WEAR, Java, and HTML5

The **smartwatch** is the next most recent consumer electronics device genre to hit the market. The smartwatch devices are also expected to explode in sales, during 2016 and 2017, primarily because there are hundreds of manufacturers manufacturing them. This is because the densely populated watch industry is moving to release smartwatch products, so that they do not lose market share to consumer electronics manufacturers, such as LGE, Sony, Motorola, and Samsung, who already have several smartwatch products each. One of the first custom Android APIs that Google ever developed was **Android WEAR** along with its **Watch Faces API**.

Digital Painting should be a popular feature that these smartwatch devices are going to support, because raster as well as vector formats can be highly optimized from a data footprint standpoint, as covered in my digital media fundamentals series. Additionally, SVG rendering is built into Android Wear hardware devices. What this means is that the smartwatch product is like an animated digital painting time piece for your users' wrists! It can provide professional digital painting and illustration, as well as asset playback results with overlayed smartwatch functionality.

This is significant for digital painting content as well as digital illustration content production and digital painting application development professionals. This is why I include it as part of this digital painting techniques title.

Another important feature of smartwatches is that you'll be able to combine your digital paint assets with other highly functional attributes, such as time, date, weather, fashion, and health features popular with smartwatches such as fitness, and physical health monitoring (heart, pulse, etc.) hardware input.

Once smartwatch screen resolutions go up from 400 pixels to 640, 800, or 960 pixels, even more functionality would become available to developers. The Huawei smartwatch already features a 400x400 pixel screen, so high resolution smartwatches should be appearing during 2016 or 2017 given that smartphones have 4K screens that are only 5 to 6 inches; so an 800 pixel smartwatch screen is certainly possible, as the technology exists already.

Smartphone and Tablet: Android, Java, and HTML5

Smartphones or **tablets** have been around the longest, as has the hybrid between the two, commonly referred to as a **phablet**. The Android OS covers all of these device types as well as personal computers that run the Android OS. There are currently billions of smartphones, as well as billions of tablets, and almost one hundred major consumer electronics manufacturers that have made products for the open source Android operating system platform.

For this reason, this represents significant opportunity for digital painting artisans and digital illustration content delivery and applications based upon both of these genres. This is because there are not as many of these digital painting or digital illustration applications as there are digital videos, digital audio, or digital imagery (photographic) applications.

All your popular smartphones and tablets include support for the lossless PNG image format, SVG command data, and for SVG XML data file formats. Modern-day devices can all render vector illustration data into raster imagery data, which will fit user device screen displays with a pixel-for-pixel precision.

Present-day content publishing platform capabilities will therefore result in very high-quality digital painting and digital illustration content consumption, and more importantly, will allow digital painting and digital illustration to be combined, not only together, but with other new media genres such as digital imaging, digital audio, digital video, and i3D. This means that you can create "never before experienced" user interface design and amazing user experiences with your digital painting artwork.

Game Console: Android, Java, JavaFX, and HTML5

Since Android, Java, JavaFX, and HTML5 now support **OpenGL ES 3.1,** a plethora of advanced game console products have appeared that are affordable priced between $50 and $100. This is yet another opportunity waiting to happen for the digital painting artisan, which you'll soon be once you practice what you learned in this book. These consoles run Android and therefore support Java and HTML5, as well as JavaFX apps or Android applications, and even e-books, for that matter. There are over a dozen brands out now.

Some major industry brands (manufacturers) are producing game controllers with Android computers inside: for instance, an nVidia Shield or GameStick. Other major manufacturers, such as Amazon, manufacture a game console iTV Set hybrid product, such as the Amazon Fire TV. Others such as OUYA and GamePop make STB (Set Top Box) products that game controllers (and iTV Set) will plug into. Some, such as OUYA and Razer ForgeTV, come with both the STB and the Game Controller, for a complete gaming package.

Since all these support Android you can utilize lossless PNG for raster digital painting components, as well as vectors, using SVG XML formats and SVG commands covered in the book, and if you use HTML5 or EPUB3 you can use PNG images, SVG commands, SVG filters, and SVG XML.

Digital painting assets can also be used inside of these OpenGL Rendering Engines that render many popular 3D games. The digital painting assets can be used for texture mapping, as can digital illustration assets.

Texture maps are applied as "skins" to 3D mesh geometry; thus 3D can take your digital illustration or digital painting content production pipelines to all new levels.

This could be done by using the open source i3D software packages, such as Blender 3D. You can download **Blender 2.76** for free, for Windows, Linux, or Mac, at http://www.blender.org today.

Future Devices: Robots, VR, and Home Appliances

The future of Android SDKs will surely bring more custom APIs. I expect to see an **Android VR,** for virtual reality goggles, as well as **Android HOME** for home appliances or home control units, and maybe even an **Android ROBOT** SDK for Android-based robots. I have already seen many of these products in the marketplace for some time so it's up to Google to provide custom APIs for these product genres, all of which will be great digital painting or digital illustration content platforms for digital illustrators and digital painters, as well as for multimedia producers and application developers who are digital illustrators and digital painters. The future is indeed bright for digital painting art!

Digital illustration as well as digital painting will be an important component in all these emerging device genres. I'd expect at least two of these genres, Home Appliances and VR, to showcase interactive digital painting as a way to increase user experience levels (VR), and because UHD home theatres will have the full attention of your viewers, comfortably seated on their couches and easy chairs.

Paid Software Platforms: iOS or Windows

The last section will cover formats that are not open source: that is, they involve paid software, and, in the case of Apple Computer, paid hardware, which will be required to develop for these platforms. Some of these require the company who owns the platform to approve (allow) your software before it can be sold in the application store. It is important to note that you will be able to get around this approval process by developing and using HTML5 for these platforms, or using JavaFX; therefore you could still deliver content for your clients without having to invest thousands in hardware (for iOS) and in software (Windows Visual C++ or C# software development packages).

There are also "hybrid" HTML5 development solutions such as PhoneGap, Cordova, and Xamarin, which allow you to develop for iOS and Windows by using an HTML5 markup and JavaScript coding work process, and these are also potential development tools for digital painting content developers to use to deliver their 2D digital painting artwork assets and content pipelines. Be sure and look into all of the programming languages and platforms in this chapter to find the one that is the best fit for you.

Apple iPhone and iPad: Supported Media Formats

As a proprietary format, Apple and iOS do not directly support SVG as all of the other platforms and devices in the world do. There are some third-party solutions and workarounds to this, like the SVGKit project on GitHub (`https://github.com/SVGKit/SVGKit`).

This is why I have focused primarily on your open source operating systems and publishing platforms for this book.

These do support the digital painting as well as digital illustration data formats, such as SVG and PNG, currently being used in Java, JavaFX, Android Studio, Kindle, HTML5, CSS3, EPUB, and JavaScript.

Windows Phone: Supported Digital Media Formats

As a proprietary format, Windows and Windows Phone also do not directly support SVG, as all of the other platforms and devices in the world do. SVG support was added in Internet Explorer 9, and there is an extension you can get for Microsoft Explorer to render SVG file thumbnails. As Microsoft and Apple represent an increasingly smaller operating system market share percentage as time goes on, this SVG format support issue will become less of a problem for digital painters and for digital illustrators.

As the free open platforms continue to gain market share percentages as time goes on, this will become less and less of an issue for digital painting professionals as well as digital illustrators. Additionally open platforms are easier to qualify and post applications and content to, and are adopted far more rapidly by the second-tier and third-tier consumer electronics manufacturers and in third world countries by using affordable platforms, such as Mozilla's Firefox OS, where devices plus OS will typically cost less than 30 dollars (or their equivalent).

Summary

In this final chapter, we took a look at digital painting and digital illustration publishing concepts, principles, platforms, and file formats that you will use to compress and decompress your digital painting and digital illustration assets, as well as to publish and distribute these to your end users. We looked at many of the different formats, platforms, and devices that will be available to you for developing digital illustration and digital painting interactive new media content.

I hope you have enjoyed this journey through the digital painting, digital illustration, layers compositing, scripting, and digital publishing concepts and work processes.

Now that you now have a fundamental knowledge of digital painting and illustration that you can build on in the future for your new media design, multimedia development, and your 2D content publishing endeavors, you can create the groundbreaking raster plus vector based application or game that can captivate users in the growing digital new media product marketplace.

Be sure to keep your eye out for my other books covering Android Studio, Java or JavaFX, HTML5, JSON, or other new media genres such as digital image compositing, digital illustration, digital audio editing, 3D, and digital video editing techniques.

Index

A

Algorithmic brush placements
  hood selection, 156
  luminosity composite method, 158
  magic wand tool, 156
  oil layer aqua layer, 157
  sketch layer and magic wand tool, 155
  soft layer composite method, 157
Alpha channels, 19, 108
Apple iPhone and iPad, 209
Arrow selection tool, 116
Audio expression, 161
  blank canvas, 162
  brush strokes, 164–165
  enable options, 163
  engine feature, 165
  information dialog, 164
  menu sequence, 162
  painting vocoder, 162

B

Blender, 15
Brush design
  blender type
    blending and color
      expression, 180
    3dRenderedCar.png, 178
    glow option, 178–179
  customization, 173
  eraser tool, 177–178
  F-X brushes
    background texture, 183–184
    dab profile image, 183
    Hurricane F-X brush variant, 182
    marbling rake, 181

overview, 173
PatternPen
  drop down selector, 175
  icon controls, 175
  Impasto brushes, 176
  Jitter algorithm, 177
  pattern palette, 174
  seamless patterns, 173
smart strokes
  acrylics dry brush, 184–185
  clone color icon, 185
  stroke preview, 186

C

Calligraphy brush stroke tool, 26
  advanced settings, 28
    caps spinner, 29
    fixation parameter, 29
    Mass setting, 29
    Thinning spinner and
      Tremor slider, 31
    tilt feature, 30
    toggle icon, 29
    Wiggle slider setting, 30
  preferences dialog, 27
  in Stroke style and
    Stroke paint, 28
Camel Impasto Cloner 2, 82
Cloning objects, 117
Codec (COde-DECode), 19
Color algorithms
  layer composite blend modes, 131
  overlay surface control effect, 131
  reflection effects, 131–132
  visual results, 132
Color sharpen images, 97

Composite layer order
    attributes, 125
    duplicate layer, 124
    ReflectionOnly layer, 123–124
Compound paths, 15
Content delivery platforms, 203
    devices, 208
    eBook Readers, 205
    EPS and PostScript, 204
    EPUB Publications 3, 205
    game console, 208
    HTML, 204
    iTV Sets, 206
    media overlay documents, 205
    open source formats, 203
    paid software platforms
        Apple iPhone and iPad, 209
        iOS/Windows, 209
        Windows and Windows
            Phone, 209
    PDF format, 204
    smartphones/tablets, 207
    smartwatch, 206–207
Corel Brush Packs
    installation, 9
    license agreement, 10
CorelDRAW, 15
Corel Painter 2016, 5
    Brush Packs, 9
    InstallShield Wizard, 5
    product updates option, 6
    in taskbar
        control panel, 8
        Pin to Start (Menu), 6

■ D

Digital computer graphics, 13
    raster concepts, 15
        alpha channels, 20
        anti-aliasing algorithms, 21
        blending modes, 20
        color depth, 18
        image aspect ratio, 16
        image resolution, 16
        picture elements, 15
        RGB color channels, 17
    vector shapes
        path, 14
        vertex, 14

Digital image compositing, 20
Digital image processing algorithms, 93
    Effects menu (see Effects menu)
Digital painting
    bitmap images
        Inkscape pattern fill, 43
        patterns, 46
        weaves, 49
    using GIMP, 39
    Inkscape styles, 37
Digital painting hardware, 53
    digital pens, 54
    driver installation
        Google Chrome, 58
        Run as Administrator, 60
    tablet
        with pressure and tilt sensitive
            stylus, 55
        with pressure and tilt stylus, 57
Digital pen, 53–54
Digital Rights Management (DRM), 204
Dynamic plug-in layers
    blending modes, 130
    CarOnlyLayer, 130
    effects layers, 127
    liquid metal dialog, 128
    ReflectionOnlyEffect layer, 129
    ReflectionOnlyPaint layer, 127–129

■ E

eBook Readers, 205
Effects menu
    color sharpen images, 97
    Highpass menu, 99
    painter algorithms, 98
    Pop Art Fill algorithm, 100
    Posterize effect, 96
    professional tablet, 93
    Sketch, 96
    stylus hardware, 93
    surface control menu, 94
    Tonal Control, 95
EPUB Publications 3 (EPUB3), 205
Eraser brush, 177–178
Esoterica submenu, 98

■ F

Filters menu, 101

■ G

Glass Distortion algorithm, 90

■ H

Highpass filter algorithm, 99
HTML5 Filters, 101
Hypertext Markup Language (HTML), 204

■ I

imageCanvas.drawBitmap() method, 195
Image Hose brush, 63
Image (layer) compositing, 19
Image pattern, 39–43
Indexed color depth, 18
Inkscape, 2, 101
    brush strokes, 25
    selections, 116, 118
    styles, 37
Invert Selection algorithm, 107
iTV Sets, 206

■ J, K

Jaggies, 21
JavaFX
    backplate layer, 191
    digital painting assets, 192
    javafx.scene.effect API, 190
    raster and vector assets, 190

■ L

Layer functions
    concepts, 119
    Inkscape
        layer menu and palette, 133
        screen blend mode, 134
    painter layers
        Alpha channel, 126–127
        color algorithms, 131–132
        compositing pipelines, 119
        drag and drop, 123–125
        effects layers, 127–130
        seamless layer elements, 120–123
Layer masks
    alpha channel, 126
    palette, 126–127
    transparency (CarOnlyLayer), and
        lock layer, 126
Lotus Petals pattern, 47

■ M

Magic wand tool, 110–111
Matching color palettes, 95
Multi-layer compositing, 66
Multimedia production
    industry, 101

■ N

Nozzles
    group layers, 74
    Image Hose, 63
    Make Nozzles from Group option, 76
    multiple layers, 66
        Brush tool, 67
        fill tool, 69
        rotate transform, 71

■ O

Overlay Composite Method, 149

■ P

Paid Software Platforms, 209
Painter 2016
    Auto-Painting feature, 32
    workflows, 31
Painter algorithms, 98
Painter patterns, 47
Painter Rainbow Pinch
    gradient, 51
Painter selections
    algorithms/wands, 105
    alpha channels, 108, 111
    channels palette, 109
    clean masked
        3D object, 115
    Eraser tool, 113
    image Luminance, 106
    Invert algorithm, 107
    Invert Selection algorithm, 107
    layer content, 114
    layer masking, 109–110
    Load From, 111
    magic wand tool, 110–111
    manual selection, 110
    menu sequence, 112
    remove black, 115
    Transform Selection, 114
    vectors, 116–117

Phablets, 53
Photographic retouching. *See*
    Photo-retouching tools
Photo-retouching tools
    ALT key, 137
    burn tool
        blemish, 143
        cleanup, 144
        color value, 141–142
        remove and twice, 144
        rubber stamp tool, 142
        saturated burn tool colors, 143
        screenshot, 141
    details editing, 135
    discolored area, 138
    dodge tool, 138–140
    rubber stamp, 136
Physics engine
    algorithm control, 161
    audio expression, 161
    digital painting vocoder
        blank canvas, 162
        brush strokes, 164–165
        enable audio expression, 163
        information dialog, 163–164
    dynamic speckle option, 169–170
    particle brushes
        animation, 165
        flow particle brushes, 167–168
        gravity, 166–167
        spring, 168
        user interface, 165–166
    RealBristle
        brush control panel, 170
        parameters, 171
Pixel blending modes, 20
Plug-In Filters
    Effects menu, 93
    SVG filters, 101–103
Pop Art Fill algorithm, 100
Portable Document format (PDF), 204
Posterize effect, 96
Pressure-sensitive stylus, 54
Programming platforms
    CSS3 and HTML5 scripting, 189
    game design
        collision polygon, 195
        command string data, 197
        spriteFrame, 197

SVG XML format, 196
    vector assets, 198
HTML5 and CSS3 markup languages
    animGIF file format, 193
    graphics elements, 193
    image composite layers, 192
    WebKit, 192
JavaFX
    backplate layer, 191
    digital painting assets, 192
    javafx.scene.effect API, 190
    raster and vector assets, 190
Painter 2016 scripting
    brush strokes, 199
    export script dialog and save
        script text, 200
    menu sequence, 198
    script options dialog, 201
    transport icons, 199
PorterDuff blending modes
    compositing pipeline, 194
    LayerDrawable, 195
    setImageBitmap() method, 195
    setXfermode() method, 195
    transfer modes, 193–194

■ Q

Quick Clone
    Blouse layer, 82
    Bristle Blender Cloner Brush, 80
    brush strokes, 88
    Camel Impasto Cloner 2, 82
    Coarse Cotton Canvas paper
        treatment, 80
    Furry Cloner brush, 85
    Hair layer, 87
    Hat layer, 86
    Magnifier tool, 84
    New Layer icon, 81
    Paper Textures drop-down, 79

■ R

RealBristle palette
    brush control panel, 170
    parameters, 171
ReflectionOnlyPaint layer, 128
Rendering, 16

■ S

Seamless layer elements
 CarOnlyLayer, 120
 cavas layer, 120
 deselect option, 123
 layer content menu, 121
 ReflectionOnly layer, 122
 save selection dialog, 122
Sketch effects, 96
Sketching techniques
 natural media brushes
  algorithmic brush
   placement, 155–158
  watercolor and liquid
   ink layers, 150, 152–155
 overlay blending mode
  Grain and Threshold setting, 148
  normal blending mode, 148–149
  overlay blend mode, 149–150
 workflow, 147
Smartphones/tablets, 207
Smartwatches, 206–207
Surface textures, 94
SVG Filter algorithms
 algorithmic processing, 103
 Inkscape, 101
 menu sequence, 102
 vector and raster objects, 101

■ T, U

Tablet plus stylus, 55
3D Bump Map, 94
Tonal control menu, 95
True Color Depth, 19
True Color plus Alpha, 19

■ V

Vector Shapes
 path, 14
 vertex, 14

■ W, X, Y, Z

Wacom, 55
Watercolor and
  liquid ink layers
 algorithmic brushing, 150
 calligraphic flat
  liquid ink, 153
 chalk layer, 154
 charcoal paper texture, 152
 layer-related
  options, 150
 paint, 152
 wine color, 154
Windows and Windows Phone, 209

Printed in the United States
By Bookmasters